THE TIMES

4TH EDITION

READY MADE JOB SEARCH LETTERS

Winning letters and e-mails to help you get your dream job

LYNN WILLIAMS

KOGAN PAGE

First Indian Edition 2009

Kogan Page India Private Limited
4737/23 Ansari Road,
Daryaganj
New Delhi 110 002

This edition is for sale in the Indian subcontinent only. Not for export elsewhere.

ISBN-10: 81-7554-476-7
ISBN-13: 978-81-7554-476-5

Published by Vinod Vasishtha for Kogan Page India Private Limited,
4737/23, Ansari Road, Daryaganj, New Delhi 110 002.

Printed and bound by Raj Press, R-3, Inderpuri, New Delhi - 110 012.

Contents

1

Job search letter basics

Why write letters?

Letters are a major part of every job search campaign. A well-written letter can:

- direct attention to your good points, and away from your weaker ones;
- give you time to work out what you want to say, and the best way to say it;
- create the right impression;
- get to people that you might not otherwise see;
- work on your behalf while you get on with something else;
- encourage people to help you;
- get your point across clearly and concisely, without interruption.

When you have a good letter, you can adapt it to use again and again.

Most people, when they think about looking for a job, think first about job application letters. There are two types of these:

1. Replies to advertised vacancies.
2. Speculative letters.

The first, as you would expect, is written in answer to advertisements inviting applications for a specific position. The second, sent to possible employers, is enquiring about suitable vacancies.

Application letters are very important, of course, but strengthen your campaign by using other types of letters as well, such as:

- requests for help or advice;
- thank-you letters;
- follow-up letters;
- reminders;
- replies to job offers;
- requests for references.

All of these follow the same basic guidelines on presentation, style and content, and you can find examples of all of them in this book. There are five key objectives to keep in mind when writing job search letters:

1. **Make a favourable impression:** Your letter will be your first contact with the company, and the impression you make at this stage will have an important effect on any prospective employer. Don't leave it until the interview to make a good impression; you may never get that opportunity.
2. **Inform**: A good application letter highlights the most important points from your CV or application form. It should underline the key details about your skills and experience that are most relevant to the job.

3. **Persuade:** Your key details, and the style and tone of your letter, should persuade the reader of your suitability for the position, and encourage them to interview you further. Write each letter specifically for the job in question. Convince the employer that you are confident you can do the job.
4. **Get an interview:** The purpose of most letters is to secure an interview with an employer, not, surprisingly, to get the job. Letters must be interesting enough for the reader to want to know more, but no letter should attempt to say everything – this is what interviews are for.
5. **Build a good relationship:** Put thought into building a good relationship with the people you write to. Use the tone and style of your letter to create a friendly impression. Consider using follow-up and thank-you letters to develop further goodwill.

Writing letters

There are three things to think about when writing letters:

1. **presentation** – the look of the letter;
2. **style** – the way you say things;
3. **content** – what you actually say.

Presentation

Your letter is the first thing about you that an employer will see. The impression that they get at this stage will stay with them, even before they actually read what you have written.

To make a good impression, your letter needs to look both professional and businesslike. Good presentation involves attention to:

- appearance;
- readability;
- layout.

Appearance

Everything you send to an employer must be immaculate, and look professional:

- Letters should be printed, unless a company specifically asks for a handwritten application.
- Use good-quality white, A4-size paper for all letters, and for your CV.
- Post CVs, application forms, and their accompanying letters unfolded in white, A4-size envelopes.
- If you send just a letter on its own, use a standard 22 cm × 11 cm white business envelope with the letter folded into three horizontally; don't fold into quarters.
- Use black ink for all writing and printing. Other colours can't be guaranteed to photocopy clearly on all types of copier.
- Never send a photocopy of a letter. Even if you are sending a standard speculative letter to several recipients, print each one separately and sign them individually.

Readability

Letters must look easy to read and inviting:

- Job search letters should be no longer than a single page, unless the circumstances are exceptional. Letters longer than this will probably duplicate what is in your CV anyway.
- Keep words, sentences and paragraphs short. Two short paragraphs are easier to read than one long one. Dense blocks of text rarely get read.

- Avoid correcting on the page. Correct your first draft before printing it out.
- Make your letter easy to read. The chances are that whoever is reading it will skim through, rather than read it word by word. Consider using bullet points for things you particularly want to stand out, such as:
  - your specific skills;
  - your main achievements;
  - your key career details.
- Use a plain, clear, easily read typeface.
- Check, and double check, spelling and grammar.

Layout

Follow a standard business letter format when writing to companies and organisations. The following suggestions will enable you to achieve a businesslike appearance:

- Write names and addresses without full stops or commas. This is in keeping with the style of layout used for the examples in this book, known as a 'block' style.
- Include the postcode on the same line as the county if you need the extra space to keep the letter to one page.
- Rather than give a string of phone numbers – home, work, mobile – put the one where you can most easily and conveniently be contacted or a message can be left. Include your e-mail address if there is a likelihood that the company will contact you via e-mail.
- Write the date in full – 12 September 2008, *not* 12/9/08 or 12th Sept. 08.
- Use the full name and title of the recipient – eg Mrs Margaret Cope – in the address line, and put their position or job title on the next line.

- Use only their title and surname in the salutation – 'Dear Mrs Cope' *not* 'Dear Margaret' or 'Dear Margaret Cope'.
- When using this block-style format, don't follow with a comma, just a one-line space before starting the main body of the letter.
- If a reference number or title appears in the job advertisement, include this in your letter at the position shown. You will notice that it is usually underlined to make it stand out more.
- With this style of layout, show paragraph breaks by using a one-line space.
- Start the first line of a new paragraph against the left-hand margin; don't indent it.
- 'Yours sincerely', your signature, and your typed name all start against the left-hand margin also.
- Because the letter is addressed to a named individual – Dear Mrs Cope – close it with the salutation 'Yours sincerely'. If you begin 'Dear Sir (or Madam)', use 'Yours faithfully' instead.
- Allow six line spaces for your signature, but reduce this if you need extra space to keep the letter to one page only.
- Type your full name under your signature. Include your title if you wish – Ann Price (Mrs).
- If you send any enclosures with your letter – your CV, references, etc – put Enc (or Encs if there is more than one) below your signature, such as Enc CV, or Encs (2).

Your address
Town
County
Postcode

Telephone number including area code
e-mail address

Full date

Full name of recipient
Job title or position
Company name
Address
Town
County
Postcode

Dear Title Surname

<u>Any reference number or title</u>

Write the main body of your letter here. ____________________

____

____

____

____

____

____

____

____

____

Yours sincerely

Your Signature

Your full name
Enc any enclosures

Style

The style of your letter – the words and phrases in which you express yourself – will tell the reader a lot about you. To create a good, professional impression, use plain English – clear, crisp and concise. Use straightforward, everyday words and phrases. Say what you mean, clearly and simply, and express yourself actively. For more about style, see Chapter 4, 'The good letter guide'.

Content

The content of the letter is the information that you give the reader about yourself. The most important thing to get across is your suitability for the job. Set out clearly and concisely your relevant skills, experience, qualities, qualifications and achievements.

For lots more about the content of your letters, see Chapter 2, 'What do I write?', and Chapter 4, 'The good letter guide'.

Now that we've looked at the basics, let's consider more closely what to actually write in the letter.

2

What do I write?

If all the important information about your skills, experience and career background is in your CV anyway, why bother with a letter as well? Isn't it just a formality saying, in effect, 'Here's my CV, hope you like it'?

In fact, your covering letter can do much, much more than that. It can:

- explain why you are sending your CV;
- clarify why you are changing jobs;
- make it clear why you're interested in this particular job;
- give details of why you are interested in working for this company;
- persuade the reader to look at your CV;
- emphasise your suitability for the job;
- highlight key elements of your background that mean you can do the job;
- demonstrate your enthusiasm and professionalism;
- supply any information they specifically ask for.

When you're looking for a job, don't lose any opportunity to make a good impression and state your case, especially not such a good opportunity as a covering letter provides. Whether you're applying for an advertised vacancy or sending your CV speculatively to companies that you hope could use your skills, make full use of your covering letter as an important element in your application, almost as important as the CV itself.

Four important paragraphs

Think of the letter as having four distinct parts:

- paragraph 1 – the opening: the reason why you are writing;
- paragraph 2 – stating your case, the reasons why you are the right person for the job;
- paragraph 3 – your reasons for applying for this job with this company;
- paragraph 4 – the closing, ending on a positive note.

Let's look at each of those paragraphs in detail.

Paragraph 1

Use your opening paragraph to say why you're writing. If you're replying to an advertised vacancy, include:

- the title of the job you're applying for and any reference number given in the ad;
- where you saw the advertisement or how you heard about the job.

If it's a speculative letter, begin by giving an immediate, topical and relevant reason for writing to the company. Why are you interested in them and why should they be interested in you?

Examples

- Ref: AA3 Divisional Manager
  I would like to apply for the above post as advertised in this month's issue of *Financial Report*. I believe I have the background and experience to make a significant contribution to XYZ Ltd in this position.
- I am writing to apply for the position of Marketing Manager as advertised in today's *Anytown Mercury*. I have extensive experience of sales and marketing and believe I have the credentials necessary for the job.
- I read on your company website about your need for a Facilities Manager. I am very interested in the position and believe that I have the skills and experience that would be of use...
- I read with interest on the current *Engineering Today* website about your new contract to manufacture XYZ engineering systems. My recent experience in this field could be of interest to you...
- I read with interest of your company's plans to open a new branch in Anytown in yesterday's *Evening Chronicle*. It occurs to me that you may have an opening for an experienced retail salesperson...
- I was very interested to learn from your website that you operate an advanced freight-handling system. As a Logistics Manager with four years' experience in...
- Congratulations on securing the new XYZ account as reported in this month's *Gazette*. As an Account Manager with experience of...

Paragraph 2

This section is the persuasive part of the letter where you say why you are right for the job and what you can contribute to the company. You are aiming to arouse the reader's interest sufficiently for them to take time to study your CV rather than just glance through it.

Highlight your most important skills, experience and achievements. If this is a speculative letter, this is also the place to outline the sort of job you're interested in.

Unless this section is very brief, splitting it into two or three shorter paragraphs will make it easier to read. Use bullet points to summarise information where appropriate – anything that makes the key points stand out and easy to read.

Examples

- I have experience of large-scale software changeover, having restructured the finance department during that time. The problems I've handled effectively include:
  - maintaining turnaround rate during departmental change;
  - designing effective training manuals;
  - taking staff successfully through the change process.

- I have been Office Manager at ABC Ltd for two years. Among the skills that will be of most interest to you are:
  - excellent staff management;
  - a first-rate record in administration;
  - proficiency at prioritising workloads;
  - the ability to implement standard procedures efficiently.

  My recent achievements include organising and supervising staff training to introduce Microsoft Office as standard across the board. This has resulted in a significant increase in both departmental and interdepartmental efficiency.

- As you will see from my CV, I have worked on an extensive range of accounts, including consumer, recruitment and financial. I have wide experience of creating exciting and imaginative publicity campaigns.
  Of particular interest to you will be the XYZ campaign, a copy of which I enclose. This prompted a response rate of 22 per cent, the highest ever achieved by the agency.

Paragraph 3

Use this section to give the employer a reason why you are applying for the job. Underline the impression that you are applying to them from choice, because of who they are and what the job is, rather than because you need a job and this one will do as well as any other. Make your reasons positive and persuasive, emphasising what you can bring to a new position, rather than what you hope they'll do for you. Concentrate on things that mean you can work at your best, such as responsibility, training opportunities, challenges, or the company's structure or reputation, and focus on the positive things you can contribute under those conditions.

Good reasons for changing your job include:

- **opportunity** – the chance to develop or do something new;
- **challenge** – more demanding responsibilities;
- **promotion** – the job you're applying for is a step up from your current one;
- **reputation** – applying to a more prestigious company.

There are other reasons for changing jobs that are just as valid but somewhat harder to defend in a covering letter. They are:

- **money** – your salary no longer reflects your value;
- **security** – you would like a more secure job with a more stable company;

- **location** – the company you're applying to is in a better or more convenient place.

Whatever reason you give, never use it as an excuse to criticise your current employer. Start by saying that you enjoy your current job and explain why, nevertheless, you want to change.

Examples

- I am presently working at the marketing organisation XYZ. However, I would very much like to return to production, where I feel my skills and experience could be used more effectively, and would welcome the opportunity this position offers to do so.
- I have enjoyed working at XYZ, and have welcomed the chance this has given me to cultivate my administrative skills. I am now, however, looking for a post with more responsibility, and feel that your advertisement offers the opportunity I am looking for.
- I am keen to find an organisation offering continued training and development, and the chance to progress in this area. I am, in consequence, very interested in the vacancy you have to offer.

Paragraph 4

End the letter with a short paragraph that closes on a positive note, confirming your interest in the job.

Examples

- I would welcome the opportunity to discuss my application with you further and look forward to hearing from you.
- I would be very happy to discuss my application with you in more detail and look forward to hearing from you.

Here are two example letters. The first is answering an advertised vacancy.

1 Sidmouth Road
Crowborough
Lincs
LN11 3FX

Tel: 00000 000000
Mobile: 00000 000000
e-mail: name@anyisp.co.uk

1 January 2009

Jane Smith
Personnel Manager
Timothy & James Ltd
141 Wellwood Road
Bassingford
Lincs
LN1 1AP

Re: Marketing Manager Ref 34 WT

Dear Ms Smith

I am writing to apply for the position of Marketing Manager as advertised in this month's *Retail Direct*. I was most interested to read your ad and believe I have the skills and experience you require.

As you will see from my CV, I have extensive marketing experience, including three years with ABC Ltd. I have a particular interest in product planning, and have successfully researched the market possibilities for several profitable new product lines.

I am at present working for DEF & Co, the product research organisation, where I have worked with the outreach team to produce excellent results. I would, however, prefer to return to consumer marketing as I believe this is where my skills and experience can be used most effectively. I am, consequently, very interested in the opportunity your vacancy offers.

I would be very happy to discuss my application with you in more detail and look forward to hearing from you in the near future.

Yours sincerely

John Brown

And here is another example letter, this time a speculative one.

19 Harbour Road
Port Ellen
Cornwall
CN11 3PU
Tel: 00000 000000
Mobile: 00000 000000
e-mail: name@anyisp.co.uk

1 January 2009

Jane Smith
Senior Staff Coordinator
XYZ Training Ltd
The Newlin Centre
Leystone
Cornwall
CN1 2TF

Dear Ms Smith

I was very interested to read about the new education initiatives for the area outlined in today's *Evening Post*, and wonder if you would have an opening for an adult literacy and numeracy teacher with counselling qualifications.

As you will see from my CV, I have considerable experience of working with people from a variety of backgrounds. I have been involved with the adult literacy scheme at the ABC Centre since its opening in 2007 as a tutor and student adviser, and I also work as a volunteer counsellor with the DEF Trust.

I have City & Guilds qualifications in both Basic Education Teaching and Practical Counselling. In addition, I have also attended GHI College's Planned Adult Literacy Course and undergone counselling training with the DEF Trust.

As the current project at the ABC Centre is drawing to a close, I am eager to continue to develop my career and make full use of my skills and experience where they would be of value. I believe your organisation could offer the opportunity to do so.

I would really appreciate the chance to discuss any suitable positions with you in more detail and look forward to hearing from you in the near future.

Yours sincerely

John Brown

3

Online letters

How the internet can help

The internet has become a major job search tool over the past few years. It offers the opportunity to:

- find out about jobs on offer;
- get information on companies and employers;
- contact potential employers swiftly;
- boost the scale and speed of your applications;
- get your CV in front of many more recruiters;
- post your CV in a variety of CV banks;
- find and apply for opportunities outside your area.

Online job hunting can be quick and convenient, but the ground rules are still the same as for any other sort of approach: a compelling covering letter attracts attention and pulls you out of the crowd.

The difference between e-mail and paper mail

Although the purpose and desired results of both are the same, there are a number of points specific to e-mail that should be taken into account:

- The screen is smaller than an A4 letter.
- E-mail is often read more quickly and with less attention.
- Your e-mail is competing for attention with many others.
- Your e-mail may need to be sent on or forwarded.
- Your CV and covering letter may initially be scanned by software rather than a person.

This means that:

- you have only a small window of opportunity in which to persuade the recruiter to go on and read your CV;
- every line counts – especially the subject line;
- key words are even more important in e-mailed covering letters than in mailed ones.

The importance of keywords

Keywords are important in all covering letters, but especially so in e-mail, where you have very little space or time to grab the reader's attention. It may not even be a human reader's attention you're trying to grab – just a computer program designed to look for specific items.

Keywords are:

- **Positions** – manager, programmer, editor, engineer, director.

- **Occupational background** – teaching, engineering, public relations, retailing, financial management, quality control, customer care, sales and marketing.
- **Knowledge areas** – capacity planning, policy and procedures, interactive technology, systems configuration, project planning, budget and resource management, MIS management, conceptual design, global markets, product development, restructuring, crisis resolution, sales and distribution.
- **Specific skills and qualifications** – Microsoft Word, Windows NT, ISO 9000, BSc, MA, two years' experience of...
- **Workplace skills** – designed, evaluated, represented, organised, formulated, developed.

The keywords in this extract from a covering letter are highlighted in bold:

> I was interested to see your opening for a Warehouse Manager – ref 337AX – on your company's website. As you will see from my CV, the position is an excellent match for my **material handling, shipping, receiving** and **warehousing** experience. In addition, I have **three years' experience in stores control** and am currently undertaking **NVQ level 2 in Wholesaling, Warehousing and Stores.**

When you send a covering letter, study the job advertisement and the job description carefully and pull out the keywords as a starting point.

Be specific

If the job description asks for word processing skills, state the specific skills you have – Word, PowerPoint, Outlook, etc. If you are, for example, a manager or a designer, say what you have managed, or what you designed.

Go into detail

If you are an IT professional with a range of skill and experience, give details of what exactly that skill and experience is:

- four years' experience in IT development;
- experience in the Unix operating system;
- worked as an ORACLE DBA;
- wrote reports using Report Writer 2x;
- worked as part of project team.

Don't forget the subject line

Always fill in the subject line of your e-mail:

- It allows the reader to see immediately who you are and what you want.
- It gives you an additional opportunity to catch the reader's attention.
- You can include some of those valuable keywords.

Keep it professional, though. If you try to intrigue or mislead with a 'teaser' subject line, you might cause irritation when the real subject of your e-mail becomes clear.

Include the job title and/or reference number if there is one, and follow with something clear and direct. You have about 60 characters to use, including spaces.

Examples

Subject: Office Manager – City Executive Assistant interested
Subject: Ref 311 Financial Administrator – FCMA 7 years' exp.
Subject: Job ref 2889 – MBA interested
Subject: Marketing exec – New York/London experience

Layout and appearance

Your details

Your name, e-mail address and the date will be at the top of the page. Start the main body of your message after this rather than taking up screen space with your home address and telephone number. Put these at the end of your message instead.

Include your e-mail address in case your letter is forwarded to someone else.

On the subject of e-mail addresses, make them as businesslike as the rest of your presentation. If yours is along the lines of partyanimal@cooldude.com, either change it or set up a separate address just for business.

Screen size

An e-mail screen is much smaller than a sheet of A4 paper. The first screen will also have subject details, your name and e-mail address at the top, leaving even less space – about 20 lines – for the key information that will make the reader want to read further. Keep this in mind when planning your letter.

Fonts

Use standard fonts and plain 11- or 12-point text for e-mailed letters and CVs. If you use a font the recipient does not have, your letter or CV could end up unreadable.

Save your word-processed covering letters in separate Rich Text files ready to be edited and pasted into e-mails when necessary.

Changing a letter – an example

Faith Harding's covering letter – see Chapter 5, *Answering advertised vacancies* – has been edited for use as an e-mail to be sent online with her CV.

Senior Project Manager
Faith Harding [fharding@anyisp.co.uk]
To: jphillips@portway.com

Dear Ms Phillips
I would like to apply for the post of Senior Project Manager (Ref 771) as detailed on Jobs.com.

I have an excellent track record in project management, particularly in information technology, having worked for some of the major companies in this field.

My achievements include:
- developing three multi-million pound projects
- increasing Nestor penetration of IT sector by 15%
- increasing the market share of Highmatch by 10%
- increasing Highmatch profits by 8%.

End of 1st screen

As well as being a skilled communicator, supportive, thorough, innovative and decisive, I also possess practical management skills, having:
- led professional teams to completion of major projects
- been responsible for commercial viability
- managed resources, including profit and loss

I look forward to discussing my application with you in more detail, and hope to hear from you in the near future. My full CV follows.

Yours sincerely
Faith Harding
3 Dean's Wharf
Pyechurch
Essex
EX3 7FV

Tel: 00000 000000

This covering letter fits comfortably on to two screens, with the most important information on the first one, giving the reader ample reason to continue to scroll down. Faith includes key words taken directly from the job posting.

General points

Just because e-mail feels more spontaneous and immediate, don't be tempted to take a more casual approach. A job-search letter demands careful thought, however it is delivered. Take the same care that you would with any other letter:

- Take time to think through what you want to say and how you want to say it.
- Check it thoroughly for spelling, grammar, etc.
- Present it as well as you would any other letter.
- Send it to the person who can make the decision.
- Send speculative letters individually and resist the temptation of Cc-ing a dozen other people with the same letter at the same time.

Your CV

It is quite likely that you will send a CV with your letter. If so, keep the following in mind.

Sending your CV as an attached file could be a problem. Many organisations won't open files from unknown sources because of the virus danger. Instead, put it in the main body of your text – save your existing word-processed CV as a Rich Text file, then copy and paste into the e-mail. Like your covering letter, you will need to edit it so it looks good on the small screen:

- Make sure it is as concise as possible. A two-page CV can run to six or seven pages on an e-mail screen.
- Arrange information in screen-sized chunks.
- Don't use bullet points, italics, etc. Some recipients can only view e-mail in plain text. Use capital letters and spacing to set out the information clearly.
- However, if are certain that your recipient can receive HTML format, then send your CV as it appears in your word-processed copy, complete with bullet points, etc.
- If you do send your CV as an attached file, remember to include your own name in the file name, as with johnsmithcv.doc. An organisation could receive several dozen files just called cv.doc.

Protecting your privacy

One drawback to online job hunting is the lack of privacy. Once you post your CV with a job bank, anyone can see it – including the company you currently work for. There are also potential problems with using workplace facilities to job-search.

If it's important that your job search remains discreet:

- Don't send e-mails from your workplace PC or have them sent to you there. (Don't do this anyway unless you have permission.) Employers can legally read your mail and track your internet use.
- Don't use your workplace e-mail address as a return address. Use your home address or set up a separate account accessible from outside.
- Most CV banks have a degree of privacy protection – password protection, visitor screening, etc. Check what your chosen site provides before enrolling.

- Don't include the name of your current employer in your CV – just put 'a major company', 'a financial organisation' or something similar.

Keeping records

Keep a record of e-mails sent and replies received, contact names and addresses and so on, just as you would with paper mail.

The good letter guide

This chapter looks at how you can turn a lacklustre letter into an interview-getting one. We'll consider the little things that can give your letter that extra bit of polish and sparkle. We'll be looking at:

- common mistakes;
- letter-writing style;
- selling your achievements.

The three worst mistakes

There are some types of letter that are almost guaranteed to turn an employer off. Unfortunately, they turn up regularly, so make sure that your own letters don't fall into any of the same traps. The three worst mistakes you can make when writing your letter are:

- oversell yourself;
- undersell yourself;
- be totally self-centred.

Fortunately, all these problems are very easy to put right with a bit of thought and preparation.

The oversell

Tony Sherman

'A born salesman'

(Unsolicited endorsement by former employer with over 20 years in sales)

3 Folly Road
Eastgate
Dundry
DN20 0AT

Tel: 00000 000000
Mobile: 00000 000000
e-mail: tonyboy@winner.co.uk

2 May 2009

Alice Gilbert
ITXL Ltd
Redbird Road
Stately
ST4 9BB

Dear Alice

LOOK NO FURTHER

Your next Sales Executive is right here. Your advertisement really grabbed my attention because I believe you can offer me a real challenge in an environment that I find incredibly energising and exciting. What's more, as you can see below, my background is an unbelievably good match with your requirements. You want it, I've got it:

IT Experience	✓
Languages	✓
International Sales	✓
B2B Experience	✓

> What your company will be getting:
>
> - A salesperson with a fantastic reputation
> - Someone with drive and ambition
> - A career-orientated professional.
>
> I will be in your area next week, so I will call you in a couple of days to arrange an interview. I know you won't be disappointed.
>
> INVEST IN YOUR COMPANY'S FUTURE TODAY!
>
> Yours
>
> *Tony Sherman*

What's right with this letter? Well:

- The writer's enthusiasm and energy shine through.
- It's short and punchy.
- Columns and bullet points make the information clear and easy to find.
- The writer is confident about what he has to offer.

Unfortunately, there's an awful lot more that's wrong with it:

- Lots of claims are made but there's no real substance to them.
- The key requirements are just ticked; no further information about what, where, when or how they've been demonstrated is given.
- No real skills or achievements are offered.
- Ringing for an interview is a bit pushy – there could be a hundred applicants all doing the same thing!

There are several technical faults with it as well that show a lack of attention to detail:

- A name is not needed at the top of the letter; the signature and printed name at the bottom will do.
- The e-mail address is less than professional.
- Alice Gilbert is given no title – Ms, Mrs, Miss – and no job title either.
- She is addressed as 'Dear Alice' instead of the more formal Ms Gilbert.
- There is a job reference number but it isn't included.
- 'Yours' rather than 'yours sincerely' is a bit too informal.
- The name isn't printed under the signature – it's no good if it can't be read.

Actually, the endorsement at the top of the page and the 'call to action' at the bottom are neither right nor wrong. It depends very much on who the letter is for, and it demands very fine judgement to gauge what the effect on any particular employer will be. If they're right for you, and for that particular job with that particular company, go ahead and use them. Otherwise, stick to a more traditional approach – but, either way, make sure you include some real meat, not just empty rhetoric.

3 Folly Road
Eastgate
Dundry
DN20 0AT

Tel: 00000 000000
Mobile: 00000 000000
e-mail: tsherman@anyisp.co.uk

2 May 2009

Ms Alice Gilbert
Sales Director
ITXL Ltd
Redbird Road
Stately
ST4 9BB

Dear Ms Gilbert

Sales Executive; your ref: IKB 3

I am writing to apply for the above position as advertised in *Sales Today*, March 19th.

Your advertisement caught my attention because I believe it offers a challenge in an area that I understand and enjoy and where my background appears to be a good match for your needs:

IT Experience	Five years' experience in IT sales with two major UK companies
Languages	Fluent bilingual German speaker with experience of business in that language, plus business-level Spanish
International Sales	Have worked in Germany, Sweden and South America for a key multinational
B2B Experience	Currently employed in business-to-business sales with a market leader

As you will see from my enclosed CV, I can also offer your company:

- 10 years' sales experience, three of them at senior management level;
- the ability to increase turnover by 37%;
- the ability to develop new market opportunities.

I would be very happy to discuss my application with you further and look forward to hearing from you.

Yours sincerely

Tony Sherman

Tony Sherman

As you can see, the improved letter gives a lot more information about Tony's very real skills and experience, all of which will be extremely interesting to any employer reading it.

The undersell

47 Park Rise
Edgecastle
EC12 7BN

Tel: 00000 000000

2 May 2009

Mr Jon Hedges
HR Manager
Faraday & Turner Ltd
Castle Business Park
Edgecastle
EC1 3TZ

Dear Sir

I would like to apply for the position of Office Supervisor as advertised in this evening's *Courier*.

I have some secretarial experience and am currently learning further office IT skills at college. I have an NVQ in Administration, although it is only a level 2 qualification. Although I have supervised staff in the past, I'm afraid it was only in a retail environment rather than an office; would this still be of interest to you?

I am currently 'just a housewife' looking after three small children, but I am very keen to get back into the workplace and hope that you will give my application some consideration. My CV is enclosed.

Yours sincerely

Molly Nunn (Mrs)

Although this letter looks totally different from the first one, and the writer comes across as a very different sort of person, the major fault is exactly the same: there's no real information. There's no incentive in either of the letters to go on and read the enclosed CV; neither look as if they have anything much to offer.

With an injection of some real substance and a little more self-confidence about what she has to offer, this letter could present a very different profile.

47 Park Rise
Edgecastle
EC12 7BN

Tel: 00000 000000
e-mail: mnunn@anyisp.co.uk

2 May 2009

Mr Jon Hedges
HR Manager
Faraday & Turner Ltd
Castle Business Park
Edgecastle
EC1 3TZ

Dear Mr Hedges

I am writing to apply for the position of Office Supervisor as advertised in this evening's Courier.

As you will see from my enclosed CV, I have four years' secretarial experience in a large export company, and am currently undertaking further office IT skills at Castleford College, including:

- Word
- Excel
- Outlook
- Access.

I have an NVQ level 2 in Administration and experience of supervising five members of staff in a busy and demanding retail environment.

Having brought up three children, I am now keen to get back into the workplace and I believe your position offers the opportunity to put my past experience and newly upgraded skills to good use.

I am very interested in this position and would welcome the opportunity to discuss it further. I look forward to hearing from you.

Yours sincerely

Molly Nunn (Mrs)

This improved version of Molly's letter puts her skills and experience across much more strongly and turns her from a no-hoper into a strong contender.

The self-centred

19 Bay View
West Clarendon
CL9 4XJ

Tel: 00000 000000
e-mail: sscott@anyisp.co.uk

2 May 2009

Ms Susan Davies
HR Manager
Smith & Foreman Ltd
West Way
Clarendon
CL1 3GD

Dear Ms Davies

I would like to apply for the position of Section Manager as advertised in this week's *Evening Post*.

I am currently a Production Controller and would welcome the chance to work as a Section Manager. Your advertisement was of particular interest to me as the position offered is exactly what I am looking for, and your company has an excellent reputation in the field of food manufacturing. I am keen to gain promotion and develop my management skills in a leading-edge company that will provide the opportunity for advancement. Your company seems to provide just that environment and I would be interested in discussing my application with you further.

I look forward to hearing from you.

Yours sincerely

Sam Scott

This letter makes it very clear what the writer is expecting the employer to do for them, but says nothing about what he will offer in return. There's no harm in sounding ambitious, but you have to let them know there's something in it for them.

19 Bay View
West Clarendon
CL9 4XJ

Tel: 00000 000000
e-mail: sscott@anyisp.co.uk

2 May 2009

Ms Susan Davies
HR Manager
Smith & Foreman Ltd
West Way
Clarendon
CL1 3GD

Dear Ms Davies

I would like to apply for the position of Section Manager as advertised in this week's *Evening Post*. I believe my skills and experience are a good match for the ones the position requires.

I am currently a Production Controller with, as you will see from my enclosed CV, five years' experience of multi-site working. During this time I have improved the process within the natural set department while reducing wastage by 35 per cent and improved efficiency overall, reducing costs and improving profit margins. I can also offer:

- extensive knowledge of the food manufacturing industry, having worked for two of the UK's leading companies;
- a thorough working knowledge of Reisenburg production systems;
- an understanding of the importance of marketability and profitability;

- staff and production supervision experience, having been shift supervisor on the production line for the past 18 months.

Your advertisement was of particular interest to me as your company has an excellent reputation in the field of food manufacturing. I am keen to gain promotion and develop my management skills in a leading-edge company that will provide the opportunity for advancement. Your company seems to provide just that environment and I would be very interested in discussing my application with you further.

I look forward to hearing from you.

Yours sincerely

Sam Scott

Sam's improved letter says a lot more about what he can offer an employer and will consequently be a lot more interesting to them.

It's not what you say, it's the way that you say it

Often, how you say something can be as important as what you say. Make your message clear and ensure you come over in the way you intend. Express yourself clearly, simply and positively. Make sure you avoid:

- outmoded business expressions;
- elaborate words, and long, involved sentences;
- stock phrases and cliches;
- modifying words such as quite, nearly and fairly;
- redundant words and phrases;
- negative phrases such as only, merely, just or but.

Outmoded business expressions

Change this:	*To this:*
As per your correspondence of the second *inst.*	In your letter of the second of September
It is the interest of the undersigned	I am interested
Enclosed herewith	Enclosed
Subsequent to	After
With reference to; with regard to; in respect of	About
Under separate cover	Separately
If you would be so kind as to	Please

Elaborate words and long, involved sentences

Change this:	*To this:*
Remuneration	Pay or salary
Ascertain	Find out
Anticipate	Expect
Terminate	End
Commencement	Start
Endeavour	Try

Keep sentences short, simple and clear.

Change this:	*To this:*
'As you can see from my attached CV, I have a degree in Social Sciences from the University of Central Mercia, and I believe that the advertised position with your organisation will give me the opportunity that I am seeking to put into effect the theoretical knowledge I have gained during the past three years.'	'As you can see from my attached CV, I have a degree in Social Sciences from the University of Central Mercia. I believe that this post will give me the opportunity to use the theory learned during the course.'

Stock phrases and clichés

Change this:	*To this:*
I think I can honestly say that I am...	I am...
Far be it from me to...	[leave this out altogether]
May I take the liberty of...	May I...
Modesty forbids me	[leave this out altogether]
Put pen to paper	Write

Modifying words such as quite, nearly and fairly

Change this:	*To this:*
I *quite* enjoyed my time there	I enjoyed my time there
The course that I have *nearly* completed	The course that I will complete at the end of January
I am *fairly* competent at planning	I am competent at planning
I was, *most of the time*, responsible for the section	I was responsible for the section

Redundant words and phrases

Change this:	*To this:*
Give assistance to	Assist
Made a purchase	Purchased/bought
Come to an agreement	Agree
Come to a conclusion	Conclude
Made a study of	Studied
Filled to capacity	Filled
Take into consideration	Consider

Negative phrases such as only, merely, just or but

Change this:	*To this:*
I'm afraid I was *just* a filing clerk	I was a filing clerk
I was *only* there for three months	I was there for three months
I have an NVQ, *but only* to level 2	I have a level 2 NVQ in...
Although I am *only* 16, I am...	I am 16, and...
I am unable to type very fast	I have a typing speed of 35 wpm

Blow your trumpet

CVs and covering letters are not the place for false modesty or hiding your light under a bushel. Use your letter to underline and highlight all the main points in your favour. If it is sufficiently interesting, the reader will happily turn to your CV or application form to fill in the details.

You need to convey to your reader a clear idea of your:

- suitability;
- benefits and achievements;
- enthusiasm.

Suitability

Set out exactly what makes you suitable for this particular job. Consider your:

- skills;
- qualifications;
- personal qualities;
- experience.

Ensure that these are things that have been asked for, or are relevant.

Benefits and achievements

Think about what you have achieved in your current, or previous, job. These needn't necessarily be outstanding career triumphs, just the everyday details of getting the job done and making steady progress.

Consider how the company has benefited from your achievements.

Workplace achievement:	*Benefit to the company:*
Achieved 80 per cent pass rate with new apprentice training scheme.	With these results, the company retained the contract to supply training.

Improved sales by 15 per cent above targets.	Helped company reach top 10 position.
Consistently delivered the highest-quality service to clients.	Maintained the excellent reputation of the organisation.

When you include your benefits and achievements in your letter, your prospective employer will see the advantages of employing you.

Most employers will be interested in anyone who can:

- **Increase**: profits, product turnover, sales, efficiency and market opportunities.
- **Decrease**: staff turnover, risks, time taken, potential problems, costs, waste.
- **Improve**: competitive advantage, appearance and/or marketability, organisation, information flow, staff performance, teamwork and relationships.

Enthusiasm

Prospective employers are pleased to see signs of enthusiasm and commitment in the letters that they receive from applicants. Show that you are interested in the job and the company, but don't be caught out giving insincere flattery. Convey the idea that, if appointed, you will do the job with energy and willingness.

Demonstrate clearly that you:

- understand the job, and can tackle it with conviction and confidence;
- understand the problems, and are equipped to handle them;
- know about the company or organisation, and appreciate its aims and ideals.

The 10 most common mistakes found in job search letters

Avoid these common errors and you will be well on your way to achieving an effective, attractive, professional letter.

1. **Not sending a covering letter in the first place.** *Always* send a letter highlighting the main points in your favour. Don't expect a prospective employer to plough through your CV or application form and work out your merits for themselves. They probably don't have the time.
2. **Dwelling on negatives.** Tell people what you *can* do, not what you can't. If you don't have the major qualifications or experience that the employer is asking for, consider whether you should be applying at all.
3. **Sending letters to a job title instead of a name, and starting 'Dear Sir or Madam'.** Always send letters, CVs and forms to named individuals. Don't leave it up to the company to decide whose responsibility it is; the chances are it will end up as nobody's. Take the trouble to find out the name and position of the person you should be writing to.
4. **Poor spelling and grammar.** If you don't take trouble over your application letter, why should they expect you to take any trouble over your job?
5. **Irrelevant information.** Unfortunately, it's tempting to put your most impressive credentials in the letter when applying for a job, even when these are not strictly relevant to the position. An employer is looking for the most suitable person for the job, not necessarily the most highly qualified. With only one page in which to make your case, get directly to the point, and leave everything else for your CV or application form.
6. **Overwritten.** Write as if you were speaking clearly and naturally to a colleague. There is no need to use special

language or elaborate phrases when writing business letters. The simpler and plainer your style, the more likely it is that your letter will be read and understood.

7. **Badly presented.** Present your letters on plain, white, good quality A4-size paper. They should be printed unless a handwritten letter is specifically asked for. Avoid ordinary small-sized writing-pad paper, coloured or patterned paper and coloured inks, as they look unprofessional.
8. **Too long.** Everything that you need to say you can usually fit on to one page – or a page and a half in exceptional circumstances.
9. **Difficult to read.** Long paragraphs, dense text and convoluted sentences make letters look unappealing. Keep your letter clear and concise, with a short, straightforward structure, and lots of white space. Use wide margins and leave a line space between short paragraphs.
10. **Inappropriate style.** Don't feel you need to adopt a 'dynamic' or 'hard sell' style of writing for your letters; the result can often seem arrogant, tactless or flippant. Stick to a friendly, natural, businesslike approach.

5

Answering advertised vacancies

General points

Reading the 'situations vacant' pages is still one of the most popular ways of looking for a new job. As well as the local and national newspapers, the best place to look for advertised vacancies is in the journals and magazines associated with your particular trade or profession.

Check the internet as well. Many newspapers and journals now offer online access to vacancies, and an increasing number of professional bodies and employers advertise job opportunities on the internet.

Before responding to an advertisement, read it through carefully, thinking about both the advertisement and the company placing it.

It is often worth phoning the company to clarify any details that you may not be sure about. Don't worry; they will be used to people doing this whenever they place an advertisement.

Study the advertisement, and ask yourself:

- **What do they want?** This should be clear from what they write, but you will probably need to read through more than once to search out all the details.
- **What have I got?** You need to know what your skills and strengths are, and which ones are relevant to this particular job.

Then match the two together.

What do they want?

The closer you can come to fulfilling the skills and experience asked for in the ad, the better. Read the ad carefully and list their requirements, the things they must have and the things they would like.

Here is an example advertisement.

> **Personal Assistant**
>
> A small natural health business in central Bristol urgently requires an experienced, mature assistant to provide administrative and secretarial support. Must have excellent organisational abilities and keyboard skills – Microsoft Office suite currently used. Good communication skills and a confident telephone manner essential as will be dealing with enquiries from the public. Knowledge of bookkeeping and familiarity with spreadsheets would be an advantage, but training will be given to the right applicant. Understanding of Fair Trade issues desirable. Must be able to work on own initiative without supervision.

Pick out the key requirements from the ad or description, then match your own skills and experience to their needs.

They want:	**I have**:
Administrative and secretarial experience	Worked as a personal assistant
Maturity – in age or attitude	Have been in responsible role in admin for over three years
The ability to organise	Organised office admin – daily running, meetings, appointments
Ability to work on own initiative without supervision	Prioritised and organised workload currently; required to deal with everyday situations on own initiative and be self-motivated
Computer skills – preferably Microsoft Office	Used Microsoft Word and Outlook at work; Excel for Environmental Group accounts
Good communication skills	Liaised with colleagues and other departments; previously worked in customer services dealing with the public – answering enquiries and offering help and advice
Confident telephone manner	Dealt with calls and enquiries to the department; customer service experience
They would prefer:	
Some bookkeeping experience	Treasurer for Environmental Group
Familiarity with spreadsheets	As above
Experience of dealing with the public	As above
Understanding of Fair Trade issues	Studied Third World economics and had first-hand experience in Africa

Once you have a clear idea of how you match the company's requirements, the covering letter practically writes itself. All you need to do is confirm that you have what they're asking for. Just take the information and organise it into a readable form.

Using a template

The following pages show a basic letter template, and the way that it can be adapted to fit the requirements of two different jobs.

The basic letter reflects the overall personality of the writer, and gives general information about them and their background that will be very similar in all cases. Into this template you can fit the key skills and qualities taken from your analysis of the advertiser's requirements. Include the key words and phrases taken from the advertisement that reflect your understanding of the advertiser's needs.

Once you have the basic template of a letter that you are happy with, you can use it every time and fit in the relevant points to suit each application.

The first letter is in reply to the advertisement on page 45 for a Personal Assistant at a natural health business. The second letter is in reply to an advertisement for someone to fill an administrative position at a consultancy. The duties include dealing with office administration, liaising with clients and promoting the company to outsiders.

10 Harding's Avenue
Somerhill
Avon
AV3 9JJ

Tel: 00000 000000

1 May 2008

Individual name
Title
Company name
Address
Address, Postcode

Dear *Name*

I am writing to apply for the position of *job title* advertised in *title and date*.

I believe I have the skills and qualities that you are asking for. I have ______________ experience, along with excellent ______________ developed through ______________.

My previous position was with McDonald Partners, where I was personal assistant to the senior partner, responsible for ______________ and ______________. This post required ______________ as well as the ability to ______________. It also, I believe, considerably developed my ______________.

Paragraph of personal details and/or specific information where appropriate.

I greatly enjoyed working in the busy office environment of McDonald Partners. Sadly, however, my job became redundant when the company was taken over at the beginning of this year. I am now looking for a position that offers the chance to ______________ and I feel that your advertisement offers just the opportunity that I am looking for.

I look forward to hearing from you in the near future.

Yours sincerely

Janice Paul
Enc CV

10 Harding's Avenue
Somerhill
Avon
AV3 9JJ

Tel: 00000 000000

1 May 2008

Mr Andrew Andrea
General manager
Whole World Health
Unit 3 Highgate Estate
Avon
AV17 5TR

Dear Mr Andrea

I am writing to apply for the position of Personal Assistant advertised in today's *Local Advertiser*.

I believe I have the skills and qualities that you are asking for. I have considerable secretarial and administrative experience, along with excellent keyboard skills, and a confident telephone manner developed through experience in customer services.

My previous position was with McDonald Partners, where I was personal assistant to the senior partner, responsible for the practical, everyday organisation and administration of the office. This post required initiative and maturity, as well as the ability to communicate effectively with people at all levels. It also, I believe, considerably developed my competence and good judgement.

I am an experienced bookkeeper, having been treasurer of the local environmental group for the past three years. My interest in environmental issues sprang from my study of Third World trade while studying economics at college, and from seeing conditions at first hand during travels in West and Central Africa. I am, consequently, a firm believer in Fair Trade policies.

I greatly enjoyed working in the busy office environment of McDonald Partners; sadly, however, my job became redundant when the company was taken over at the beginning of this year. I am now looking for a position that offers the chance to become closely involved with a thriving organisation once again. I feel that your advertisement offers just the opportunity that I am looking for.

I look forward to hearing from you in the near future.

Yours sincerely

Janice Paul
Enc CV

---

10 Harding's Avenue
Somerhill
Avon
AV3 9JJ

Tel; 00000 000000

1 May 2008

Ms Jo Hillier
Centre Manager
The Argos Consultancy
6 Green Court
Pudsey
Avon
AV8 1PO

Dear Ms Hillier

I am writing to apply for the Administrative Position advertised in today's *Local Advertiser*.

I believe I have the skills and qualities that you are asking for. I have considerable administrative experience, along with excellent presentation skills, both verbal and written, developed through experience in client services and liaison.

My most recent position was with McDonald Partners, where I was personal assistant to the senior partner, responsible for the practical administration of the office. This post required accuracy and dependability, as well as the ability to communicate effectively with people at all levels. It also considerably developed my qualities of resourcefulness and initiative.

While there, one of my most agreeable duties was to organise business and social functions for both clients and suppliers. I arranged a total of 14 such functions during this time, which, I believe, provided satisfaction and enjoyment for all concerned.

I greatly enjoyed working in the busy office environment of McDonald Partners; sadly, however, my job became redundant when the company was taken over at the beginning of this year. I am now looking for a position that offers the chance to put my administrative skills to good use with an expanding company. I feel that your advertisement offers just the opportunity that I am looking for.

I look forward to hearing from you in the near future.

Yours sincerely

Janice Paul
Enc CV

Examples

The following letters are all answers to advertised vacancies. If you look at them closely, you can see that each of them has a different basic framework into which you could insert your relevant skills, qualities and qualifications. For example, the basic template of Linda's e-mail is as follows.

I would like to apply for the position of ____________________
as advertised in ________________.

As you will see from my career details, I have extensive experience of ______________________ including:

- ____________________
- ____________________
- ____________________
- ____________________

I am currently employed at _________________ where my most recent achievement has been to __________________. The resulting benefit to the company was __________.

I enjoy _____________________. I see it as my responsibility/role/duty to _____________.
I believe that your vacancy offers the opportunity I am looking for to ___________. My aim is to ______________.
I would be very happy to discuss my application with you further and look forward to hearing from you.
My full CV follows.

The specific skills and qualities that Linda has selected are the result of matching the needs that Anchorage Inns expressed in their advertisement, with the qualities and experience that she has.

Note that all the letters are very positive and concentrate on the applicants' strengths, rather than on their shortcomings. The tone of the letters, overall, is polite and businesslike, and each puts its best points forward well. The writers sound assured without being pushy or boastful.

Catering Manager Application
Linda Vernon [lvernon@anyisp.co.uk]
To: pcox@anchorinns.com

Dear Mr Cox

I would like to apply for the position of Deputy Catering Manager as advertised on this month's Hotel and Catering website.

As you will see from my career details, I have extensive experience of both catering and catering management, including:

- two years as assistant manager at a leading upmarket restaurant
- two years as assistant manager to a commercial catering company
- catering supply manager for a large northwest hospital trust for three years
- four years' general experience in the restaurant and catering trade.

I am currently employed at La Noisette restaurant, where my most recent achievement has been to oversee the systematic organisation of staff training schedules. The resulting decrease in staff turnover of nearly 20 per cent greatly improved the standard of service we were able to offer customers.

I enjoy creating an atmosphere in which people can have a good time without worries or distractions. I see it as my responsibility to ensure that everything runs smoothly, and I understand the challenge of remaining calm and efficient under pressure.

I believe that your vacancy offers the opportunity I am looking for to work in the fast-growing family entertainment market. My aim is to develop my career further in the area of first-rate customer service, both personally and through staff management and motivation.

I would be very happy to discuss my application with you further and look forward to hearing from you.

My full CV follows.

Yours sincerely

Linda Vernon
21 Oldsbury Court
Elmdale
Essex
EL14 4RJ
lvernon@anyisp.co.uk
Tel: 00000 000000

5 Windmill Court
Sellingsby
Birmingham
BM19 3JK

Tel: 0000 000 0000

14 July 2008

Ms J K Allison
Head of Personnel
Ross College
Warwickshire
WW11 2DC

Dear Ms Allison

Ref: UER/3/AO, Accommodation and Welfare Manager

I am writing in answer to your advertisement in today's *Bowerfield Post and Chronicle* requesting applications for the position of Accommodation and Welfare Manager for undergraduate students.

I believe I have the skills and qualities that you are looking for. I have considerable experience of working with people to solve their housing problems. I currently work for the Broadham Trust as Housing Officer, giving advice and support to those in housing need, as well as undertaking the practical organisation of accommodation.

I have a thorough understanding of housing and tenancy legislation, and environmental health legislation. I also have additional experience of housing benefit rights and entitlements.

I have greatly enjoyed my work with the Trust, where my greatest achievement to date has been to develop a successful programme of inner city accommodation provision for young ex-offenders.

I am keen to find an organisation offering continuing training and the chance to progress in this most stimulating field. I am, as a consequence, very interested in the vacancy that you have to offer.

I would welcome the opportunity to discuss my application with you further and hope to hear from you in the near future.

Yours sincerely

Andrew Patterson
Enc CV

3 Dean's Wharf
Pyechurch
Essex
EX3 7FV

Tel: 00000 000000
e-mail: fharding@anyisp.com

6 August 2008

Ms Tina Irwin
Recruitment Manager
DDS
PO Box 3
London
SW4 9KK

Dear Ms Irwin

Please find enclosed my CV in application for the position of Senior Project Manager as advertised in this week's *Business Brief.*

I believe I have the character and experience that you are looking for. I have an excellent track record in project management and particularly in information technology, having worked for some of the major companies in this field.

I am a skilled communicator – supportive and thorough, as well as innovative and decisive. In addition to inter-personal skills, I also have practical management skills. I have managed group resources, including profit and loss accountability, and been responsible for the commercial viability of team projects with my previous employers, Highmatch.

As you will see from my enclosed CV, I am currently employed by Nestor plc. My aim there is to provide the motivational and management skills needed to lead a professional team through to completion of a major project.

My achievements to date include initiating and developing three highly successful multi-million-pound developments:

- increasing the penetration of Nestor within the IT sector by 15 per cent;
- increasing the market share of Highmatch by 10 per cent;
- increasing Highmatch profits by 8 per cent.

As the current project is now drawing to an end, I am eager to continue to develop my career and feel certain that your position offers the opportunity to do so.

I very much look forward to discussing my application with you in more detail, and I hope to hear from you in the near future.

Yours sincerely

Faith Harding (Ms)
Enc CV

27 January 2008

Mrs Paula Wing
Personnel Manager
Apex Group
Apex House
Ringway
Berkshire
BK2 2OL

Dear Mrs Wing

Ref: JJ/9/SSB Personal Assistant

I am writing to apply for the above post as advertised in today's issue of the *Evening Echo*, as I believe I have the skills and experience you require.

As you will see from my enclosed CV, I have thorough experience of this type of work. This includes two years as administrative assistant at ISP International, and three years as personal secretary to the Personnel Director at Service plc.

My computer skills include Word, Access and Outlook, and I have RSA grade III typing and clerical qualifications.

My current position as secretary to a Housing Management team requires initiative and self-confidence, as well as the ability to communicate effectively with people at all levels. While in this position, I believe I have also developed my qualities as a team worker. My most recent success has been to organise the details of this year's Housing Conference to the complete satisfaction of all those taking part.

I have enjoyed working in a busy office environment, and I have welcomed the opportunity this has given me to cultivate my aptitude for prioritisation and organisation. I am now, however, looking for a post with more responsibility, and feel that your advertisement offers just the opportunity that I am looking for.

Thank you for considering my application. I look forward to hearing from you in the near future.

Yours sincerely

Angela Price
Enc CV

9 Bread Street
Crofthouse
Cardiff
CF9 9OK

Tel: 000 0000 0000
e-mail: alderk@anyisp.com

30 July 2008

Mrs Sarah Kent
Personnel Manager
Westhope Food Industries Ltd
West Dock, Rivershead
CF25 8SA

Dear Mrs Kent

Ref. 09/K/LT3, Laboratory Technician

I am writing to apply for the position of Laboratory Technician advertised in this week's *Journal.*

As a fully qualified food technician with an HNC in General Science, I believe I fit your requirements.

As you will see from my enclosed CV, I am currently employed at Parkway Products plc, where my greatest success to date has been the successful completion of improved production trials. When brought into operation, these will result in an estimated saving to the company of over £50,000 a year.

I am organised and dependable, also quick-thinking, with a lively interest in scientific matters. I am currently very interested in recent developments in the food industry – in particular, the enhanced methods of food-spoilage prevention.

I would, therefore, greatly appreciate the opportunity that this position offers to become involved with this subject at a practical level.

I am confident that I could make a valuable contribution to Cedar House Foods in the position advertised, and I would welcome further discussion of my application. I look forward to hearing from you.

Yours sincerely

Katherine Alder (Miss)
Enc CV

Chief Financial Officer
MBFA Interested
Jonathan McEean [jmceean@anyisp.co.uk]

To: njgold@dannholdings.com

Dear Mr Gold

I have recently completed the Institute of Financial Management MBFA through South City University and I am interested in applying for the position of Chief Finance Officer advertised on this month's Business Analyst recruitment board.

My experience as both an accountant and a financial administrator makes me, I believe, well qualified for the post. My background includes:

- finance manager for Hall Holdings industrial division;
- five years as audit supervisor with Collins & Hodge;
- accountant and financial administrator with the largest haulage company in Europe;
- staff accountant for D-C Services Ltd.

Recent successes include the profitable renegotiation of credit facilities at Hall Holdings, and the implementation of a freight cost analysis, which resulted in an annual saving to the organisation of over £150,000.

I am an energetic, ambitious professional, with a decisive, self-reliant personality. I am also well able to work co-operatively and productively within a team environment.

Although I have been very happy with Hall Holdings, I am now looking for a position that will allow me to use the skills and competencies that I have acquired through my recent MBFA. I believe that your vacancy offers just the opportunity that I am looking for in order to advance my career.

I would very much appreciate learning more about Vann Dannhouse and its objectives. I am currently available for interview at any time and I look forward to hearing from you.

My full CV follows.

Yours sincerely

Jonathan McEean
6 Ellery Gardens
North Axely
Surrey
SY3 4AZ
jmceean@anyisp.co.uk
Tel: 00000 000000

5 Southway Road
East Studley
Surrey
ST6 7WS

Tel: 00000 000000

3 June 2008

Ms E L Harper
Manager
Ellenby Foods
Trident Way
South Shelby
Surrey
SU7 9TZ

Dear Ms Harper

Ref: PMM/ELH/17

I am applying for the position of Planning Manager (Marketing) advertised in the *Grocery and Provisions Gazette*, issue number 6, June 2008.

As my CV shows, I have extensive marketing experience, including three years with Cabot Confectionery. I have a particular interest in product planning, and have researched the market possibilities for several successful new product lines.

At present I am working for JBL, the research and consumer survey organisation. I would very much like to return to consumer marketing, however, and would welcome the opportunity that your vacancy offers to do so.

I look forward to hearing from you.

Yours sincerely

Jonathan McInnery
Enc CV

Application form request

When an advertisement asks you to write for further information, or for an application form, this is all that you need to do.

The organisation may have several vacancies open at any one time. In order to make sure that you get details of the one that interests you, it is important to include:

- the title of the vacancy you are applying for;
- any reference number given in the advertisement;
- the date and publication in which the vacancy was advertised;
- a request for the company to forward an application form and job description.

The letter is a straightforward request for further information.

When you return the completed application form, that is the time to include your detailed covering letter highlighting your suitability for the post.

43 St. John's Road
Adrington
Wiltshire
AD14 7QU

Tel: 00000 000000

16 July 2008

Mr E Hill
Personnel Officer
Ling Wholesale
West Park
Exeter
EX10 9ED

Dear Mr Hill

Ref. SS/122/B/3

Please could you send me an application form and further details of the vacancy for warehouse supervisor as advertised in the *Exeter Post*, 15 July 2008.

Yours sincerely

Michael Coleman

6

Speculative letters

General points

Many jobs are never actually advertised. Some estimates say that these may amount to between 60 and 70 per cent of all positions available. The organisations concerned either already have someone in mind for the job, or have a good selection of candidates who have already sent in their CV 'on the off-chance'.

Because of this, it is well worth making speculative approaches to companies – sending them your CV and a covering letter even though they aren't currently advertising for staff. Send speculative letters to companies to let them know who you are and what you can do. Although a speculative letter often accompanies a CV, its emphasis is slightly different from the covering letter sent with your CV in answer to an advertisement.

The aim of a speculative letter is to get an interview with the person you are writing to. This may be an informal interview for you to get more information about the company and their requirements, or it may be an interview for a specific job.

There is no readily available job description to work from as there would be with an advertised vacancy. Therefore, you need to do some research in order to compile a speculative letter that will get the attention that it deserves.

First, you will need to find the names and addresses of suitable companies to write to. Then you will need to have some information about the companies themselves.

When you are looking for a new job, it helps to know as much as possible about your field of work. This is especially true when you are making speculative applications. All the information may not be immediately useful to you, but everything you know helps to build the overall picture. This will increase your confidence and help you to find your way around until, one day, you 'just happen' to be in the right place at the right time.

What do you need to know?

Make sure that you know:

- what's happening in your field of work;
- what's changed in that field recently;
- what's new, what's coming up in the future;
- which companies do your type of work or need it done for them;
- what they do – whether it is the same as you are used to doing or there are differences;
- who they are, what their background is, organisational structure, reputation;
- where they are heading, what's new for them;
- who's moving into the area;
- who's expanding, who's tendering for contracts;
- who are the key people to contact within these organisations.

Sources of information

General reading

- Local newspapers;
- National newspapers;
- General interest magazines.

These will have news, features and articles on businesses, new products and services, exhibitions and events, special promotions, community issues, company expansion or relocation, building and site development.

'Situations vacant' pages in local or national papers and in trade journals will also give you an idea of what the job market is like.

Trade and business publications

- Trade journals;
- Company newsletters;
- Annual reports and financial reports.

Virtually every type of job has its own newspaper or journal that will tell you what is happening. Many of them also include 'situations vacant' pages. Company newsletters and annual reports will give you more specific information about companies. You can obtain them from the company by writing in.

Trade and business directories will give you information about specific companies, from their names and addresses to the number of people that they employ. There are also directories that will tell you about professional or trade associations, and trade-related journals and publications.

The internet

Many of the publications mentioned above are now available on the internet. In addition, you should be able to find:

- Company websites;
- News and chat groups;
- Professional organisations' and societies' websites;
- College and university careers pages;
- Career guidance sites;
- Recruitment agency sites.

These will give you detailed factual information as well as background data on your chosen area both for your own country and abroad. Career guidance and recruitment sites often carry ideas about labour market trends, employment profiles, recruitment events, etc, as well as giving specific information on jobs.

People

- Current and former colleagues;
- Customers, suppliers and business contacts;
- Professional and trade associations;
- Careers advice services;
- Employment agencies and headhunters.

The more people you contact, the more likely you are to find that perfect job. Even if people can't help you directly, they can often put you in touch with someone who can.

One of the best places to start looking for information is your public library. Here you should be able to find many of the directories, journals and other publications mentioned above, as well as online access. The staff should also be able to help you find out about professional associations and other organisations that may be helpful to you.

Writing a speculative letter

There are two things that greatly help the success of a speculative letter, and increase your chances of getting an interview:

- Always send the letter to a named individual in the organisation, not just to 'The Personnel Department' or 'The HR Manager'.
- Always follow up your letter with a telephone call to make personal contact.

A speculative letter usually follows the same format as the one outlined in Chapter 2. To recap:

- **The opening gambit:** A brief paragraph that gives your reason for writing to this particular company at this particular time. The more topical, immediate and relevant you can make this section, the better.
- **The persuasive section:** The main body of the letter outlining how, exactly, you can contribute to this particular company at this particular time, and conveying the benefit to them of employing you. State the sort of position in which you are interested, include your most relevant skills and experience, and highlight your achievements. This section can be two or three short paragraphs, instead of one long one, in order to make reading it easier.
- **The reasons** why you want to work for this particular company.
- **The closing paragraph:** A short paragraph emphasising your interest in the job, mentioning any enclosures such as

your CV if you haven't already, and stating what your follow-up will be, ie 'I will call early next week to request a short meeting', or 'I will contact you shortly to discuss this further'.

Broadcast letters and topical letters

Speculative letters fall into two major categories:

- **Broadcast letters:** These contain rather generalised information about your skills and strengths. Their advantage is that, as they are general, you can send them out to all the companies that employ people doing your sort of job. They can also be e-mailed to a large number of companies.
- **Topical letters:** These are individual letters written to specific companies. Topical letters, as their name suggests, are prompted by current events such as the company being in the news, or a meeting with a member of the organisation. As each letter is aimed at an individual company and written especially for them, these letters take longer to prepare than broadcast letters. But, even though they may take more effort, they are worth the trouble. Being more personal, they do get a much better response than broadcast letters.

Examples of both these types of letters can be found on the following pages.

Speculative letters can be e-mailed to companies, and broadcast letters in particular can be e-mailed to a large number of organisations quickly and cheaply. However, different sectors currently have different reactions to being contacted in this way. Know your own industry and use your judgement. Be aware that there is probably a greater chance that your e-mailed details will *not* be filed and kept than if you had sent a hard copy.

Broadcast letters: the administrator

Allison is looking for a job as an administrator or office manager with a big organisation. She is sending out speculative letters to all companies over a certain size within reasonable commuting distance. There are a lot of these companies, so Allison has decided to forgo targeted topical letters, which would mean researching each one individually. Instead, because the job she is looking for will be reasonably similar in any company, Allison is able to send out a standard broadcast letter to each, listing her main strengths and skills. She can, in addition, send topical letters to those companies about which she has more information, or some knowledge or personal contact.

- Even though she is sending her broadcast letter out to dozens of prospective employers, Allison takes the trouble to call each company and find out the name of the right person to send it to.
- She opens the main body of her letter with her background and her present position. This gives the reader a good idea of her current level of responsibility and indicates what she is looking for. She has already said that she is hoping to further her career, and would, presumably, want to improve on this.
- Allison knows the job well and is very clear about what is required of a good administrator. She can, therefore, make an educated guess about what the company will want and include these key qualities in her letter.
- She lists her specific skills separately, which makes them stand out more.
- She closes the main part of the letter with an emphasis on her most recent achievements with her current employer. Her ability to improve efficiency would be of interest to most organisations.
- Allison finishes with a request for a meeting. She makes it clear that she will follow up her letter, demonstrating her

enthusiasm and commitment, as well as her initiative for writing in the first place. To see how Allison follows up this letter at a later date, see Chapter 13, *Follow-up letters*.

For the result of another of Allison's speculative letters, see Chapter 16, *Answering job offers*.

Ash Cottage
Tovey Lane
Tillington
Berkshire
BR17 4DF

Tel: 00000 000000

7 March 2009

Mr Kevin Walker
Personnel Director
Willings & South
Terrence Place
London
EC1 1FF

Dear Mr Walker

I am hoping to further my career in administration and office management. I am writing to you to ask if you have any vacancies in this area at present, or whether you might have any in the near future.

As you will see from my enclosed CV, I have an extensive knowledge of the field, including four years as an office supervisor, and seven years in general administration. My current position is with Read-Hall Assurance, where I am responsible for a department of 25 staff dealing with the collation and administration of all documentation and records for the company.

I am a good communicator, who has demonstrated a high degree of initiative and self-motivation. I enjoy the challenge of a busy, demanding work environment, and I am conscientious, with the ability to maintain a consistently high standard of work under pressure. The skills and experience that I have which would be of particular interest to you include:

- good staff management skills;
- an excellent track record in administration;
- proficiency at prioritising workloads;
- the ability to implement standard procedures correctly and efficiently.

My recent achievements include organising and supervising training for staff to integrate Microsoft Office applications. This resulted in a significant increase in departmental efficiency.

I would welcome the opportunity to discuss how I could contribute to the continued success of your organisation and will call within the week to arrange an appointment. I look forward to speaking with you.

Yours sincerely

Allison Tripp
Enc CV

Broadcast letters: the sales manager

Like Allison, Michael is sending out a lot of letters to companies who may be interested in his skills as a sales manager.

This letter is one of three that Michael has prepared, each aimed at one of the main areas in which he has experience as a sales executive: financial services, consultancy services and media sales.

18 Clementine Square
High Grange
Surrey
SR23 9CS

Tel: 00000 000000

3 September 2008

Ms Maria Derby
Sales Director
Bower-Peal Financial Services
Columbus Way
London
W4 7HH

Dear Ms Derby

I am currently looking for a position in the finance sector, and am writing to you to enquire whether you have any suitable vacancies for an experienced sales manager.

I am dependable and energetic, with the ability to motivate and direct a sales force to meet targets and objectives. I am skilled at building customer loyalty and have developed, through experience, a highly competent level of management and organisational skills.

Areas of specific experience that will be of interest to you include:

- responsibility for annual sales increase of nearly 30 per cent over five years;
- overall responsibility for four major product launches in as many years;
- formulation of policy at all stages of sales development;
- successful initiation and organisation of sales training programmes;
- personal track record in direct sales with a large client base.

As you will see from my enclosed CV, I have a strong background in financial services as well as sales and I believe that I could make a significant contribution to your organisation.

I would really appreciate the opportunity of a short meeting with you to discuss possible openings, and will contact your office within the next few days to request a suitably convenient date and time.

Yours sincerely

Michael Franks
Enc CV

- By changing the words 'finance sector' and 'financial services' in the first and last-but-one paragraphs respectively, Michael can easily change this letter from one aimed at financial organisations to one that draws on his experience in other industries. As a result, although this is a broadcast letter, it is still possible to target it to some extent, making it a little more relevant to the reader. This idea is expanded still further in the next two letters.
- Michael has a very clear picture of what makes a good sales manager, and he is able to include these qualities in his letter. He shows that he appreciates the important requirements for the position: the ability to build customer loyalty and to motivate staff to meet targets and achieve sales.
- He picks out his specific areas of experience and lists these separately to highlight them. This makes it easier for the reader to get an idea of what his capabilities are.
- He has included his achievements with his areas of experience. Most companies would be interested in someone who has the ability to increase sales by nearly 30 per cent.

Different broadcast letters for different jobs: the adult literacy tutor and the counsellor

These two letters, although essentially the same, appear to be very different. Each highlights different skills and qualities relevant to the position that Marcie is applying for.

Marcie is well qualified to do two different jobs and has, therefore, decided not to list all her skills and qualifications in one letter. Instead of leaving it to the reader to decide what sort of work she is able to do, Marcie is sending out two different broadcast letters to organisations that may be interested in her skills.

Both the following letters written by Marcie are based on a basic template as explained in Chapter 5. The basic template is as follows.

> I am writing to you regarding any employment opportunities that ____________ may have for a ____________________.
>
> As you will see from my enclosed CV, I have had considerable experience of working with people from a variety of different backgrounds. I am a ________________ who is skilled at ___________.
>
> *Paragraph on specific working experience.*
>
> My relevant qualifications include ___________________. In addition to these, I have also ___________ and __________.
>
> I believe that my skills and experience could be of value to you and would welcome the opportunity to discuss this with you further. I will call your office within the next few days to see if we can arrange a suitably convenient date and time.

- Into this framework she has put the skills, qualifications and characteristics suitable for each of the two different types of job she can do – adult literacy teaching, and counselling. Marcie knows enough about both jobs to be able to make an educated guess as to what a prospective employer would be looking for, and to include these points in her letters.
- She shows that she understands what each job is likely to entail – having to work with people very different from herself from a variety of backgrounds, patience, perception, etc.
- The paragraph in each letter that is the most different in each case is the one where she outlines her actual experience. Each one is specifically relevant to the position in question. Marcie has been selective, and has not been tempted to put in everything, or to give all her experience equal importance.
- Note how, although she has included the same qualifications in each letter, she has put the most relevant qualification first in each case. Her teaching certificate goes first for the teaching post, and her counselling certificate first for the counselling post.
- Note too, the different emphasis given to her additional training in each letter.
- It is very easy to tell from each of these letters exactly what sort of post Marcie is interested in, together with how well qualified and experienced she is to do it. Had she tried to combine all her experience into one, this might not have come out so strongly or so clearly.
- Marcie also has two different versions of her CV. Although they both have the same basic information in them, like the letters, each highlights different qualifications and experience.

12 April 2008

Mr Bernard White
Staff Co-ordinator
Owerby Education Service
Tibbs Green
Owerby
Lincolnshire
LN3 9WE

Dear Mr White

I am writing to you regarding any employment opportunities that Owerby Education Service may have for a trained literacy and numeracy teacher with counselling qualifications.

As you will see from my enclosed CV, I have had considerable experience of working with people from a variety of different backgrounds. I am a patient and perceptive tutor who is skilled at establishing rapport with others and enjoys doing so.

I have been involved with the adult literacy scheme at Spring Gardens Open Access Centre since its opening in 2003, first as an administrator, and currently as a tutor and student counsellor. I also work as a volunteer counsellor with the St Martin's helpline.

My relevant qualifications include City & Guilds 3713 Basic Education Teaching, and RSA Practical Counselling Certificate. In addition to these, I have also attended Redhill College's Planned Adult Literacy course, and undergone counselling training for the St Martin's Trust.

I believe that my skills and experience could be of value to you and would welcome the opportunity to discuss this with you further. I will call your office within the next few days to see if we can arrange a suitably convenient date and time.

Yours sincerely

Marcie MacBride (Mrs)
Enc CV

8 Ridgway
Owerby
Lincolnshire
LN7 1JM

Tel: 00000 000000

12 April 2008

Mrs Rita Viatta
Personnel Manager
Owerby Health Trust
PO Box 99
Owerby
LN99 3HO

Dear Mrs Viatta

I am writing to you regarding any employment opportunities that Owerby Health Service may have for a qualified counsellor.

As you will see from my enclosed CV, I have had considerable experience of working with people from a variety of different backgrounds. I am a patient and perceptive communicator who is skilled at establishing rapport with others and enjoys doing so.

I am currently working as a counsellor and supervisor for the St Martin's helpline. This, as you will know, is the counselling service for young people facing crisis in the home. I have been with them for over three years, both as a telephone counsellor and as a one-to-one befriender. I am also a student counsellor and tutor for the Spring Gardens Open Access Centre, working with people who have literacy problems.

My relevant qualifications include the RSA Practical Counselling Certificate, and City & Guilds 3713 Basic Education Teaching. In addition to these, I have also undergone counselling training for the St Martin's Trust, and attended Redhill College's Planned Adult Literacy course.

I believe that my skills and experience could be of value to you and would welcome the opportunity to discuss this with you further. I will call your office within the next few days to see if we can arrange a suitably convenient date and time.

Yours sincerely

Marcie MacBride (Mrs)
Enc CV

Topical letters prompted by information in the news

- Elinore's speculative letter has been suggested by a piece that she has read in her local paper about a college's planned expansion on to a new site.
- She has thought about what this expansion will mean to the college in terms of increased workload, and offered her services accordingly. This in itself shows that Elinore has initiative and intelligence, and fully understands the pressures and problems facing a large organisation.
- Note that she is clearly offering to help the college with their problem – their increased administration needs – rather than asking them to help with her own – her need of a job.
- Elinore is also able to offer specific experience with a database system similar to the one the college is introducing. This, again, shows that she understands the problems that they have. They will need someone familiar with the system who can use it, and someone who can either train other people to do so, or who can arrange training for them.
- Elinore doesn't go into great detail about her general skills and experience. She concentrates exclusively on the specific points raised by the newspaper article, and emphasises where she can help with these.
- Her letter is sufficiently interesting and relevant for Mr Frobisher to take the trouble to look up her other career details in her enclosed CV.

192 Paulton Road
Westwell
Hertfordshire
HE19 7XZ
Tel: 00000 000000

28 January 2008

Mr P S Frobisher
Personnel Director
Whiteside College of Further Education
Watford Road
Springdale
Leeds
LD6 4LJ

Dear Mr Frobisher

I read with interest of your college's plans to expand on to the new site at Addendale in yesterday's *Leeds Chronicle*.

It occurs to me that due to the projected large increases in administration, you may have an opening for someone with my career record.

As my enclosed CV will show you, I have in-depth experience on the administrative staff of a large college, and am well versed in organisation and management. You may be particularly interested in my experience with the introduction of an extensive new database system similar to the one outlined in the newspaper article. I have, in addition, experience of staff training in connection with this.

I would welcome the opportunity to discuss how my skills and experience could contribute to the continued efficient running of the college and will call within the week to arrange an appointment. I look forward to meeting you.

Yours sincerely

Elinore Downs
Enc CV

Topical letters prompted by an item in the specialist press

This e-mail was prompted by a news item on the website of the professional journal that Angus reads. The fact that he reads the specialist publications with such attention and interest is already a point in his favour.

- Note that Angus comes straight to the point. The first paragraph gives his reason for writing at this time.

> Antigenic enzyme experience offered
> Angus Hanshaw [ahanshaw@anyisp.co.uk]
> To: acarter@korepharm.com
>
> Dear Mrs Carter
>
> I read on the current Pharmacy website about your new contract for manufacturing Antigenic B+ lipoenzyme test systems. Congratulations on securing such a valuable order.
>
> I have worked on the development of similar antigenic systems for the L&K Corporation in Swindon, and feel that this experience could make a substantial and immediate contribution to you at this time. Details are in the following CV.
>
> I would welcome the opportunity to discuss this with you, some time next week if possible. I'll contact you shortly to arrange a possible meeting time.
>
> My full CV follows.
>
> Yours sincerely
>
> Angus Hanshaw
> 43 Bowes Lane
> Edinburgh
> EH5 4PQ
> ahanshaw@anyisp.co.uk
> Tel: 0000 000 0000

- Like Elinore, Angus has concentrated specifically on the most important thing that he can offer – his experience with the development of a similar system. He stresses the substantial and immediate contribution he could make to the company.
- He directs the reader to his CV for the details of his career. To include them in his letter would make his main strength – his experience – far less clear.
- Such experience could be of enormous value to a company setting up a new operation. It could help them to cut down on the time it takes to start up production, and it might prevent some of the common 'teething problems' they will be anticipating.
- By e-mailing the company in this way, Angus demonstrates that he has initiative and intelligence, and that he fully understands the pressures and problems facing the organisation.

Topical letters prompted by a meeting at an event

This letter follows up a meeting at a business exhibition. Rather than pursue the matter in the busy atmosphere of the exhibition, Sam has written to Julian Vell afterwards.

- Sam opens with a reminder of their meeting so that Julian Vell will be able to place who she is. It is unlikely that he will remember her name alone after a fairly brief and casual conversation.
- She has thought over what they talked about, and what this will mean to Astra in terms of the problems they may encounter. She is offering her expertise accordingly. This in itself shows that Sam has initiative and intelligence, and fully understands the pressures and problems that accompany such large-scale introductions.
- Sam sets out the specific obstacles that she thinks they will face. This, again, shows that she understands the problems, and clearly demonstrates her previous experience.

- She doesn't go into detail about her general skills and experience. She concentrates exclusively on the specific points that will interest Astra, and emphasises how she can help.
- If Julian Vell wants to know more detail, her letter is sufficiently interesting and relevant for him to take the trouble to meet her for a further discussion.

Flat 2
Ibbstone Court
Torbey Road
Torbey
Leicester
LE3 6DD

Tel: 0000 000 0000
e-mail: samtar@anyisp.com

14 August 2008

Mr Julian Vell
Astra Finance
Astra House
Wellings Road
Derby
DB9 7HW

Dear Mr Vell

It was really nice to meet you at the recent *Business Software Now* exhibition and hear about the recent developments at Astra Finance.

I was interested to learn that your company is considering introducing PDR intranet systems into all its subsidiary offices to facilitate the use of high-turnover accounts packages.

As you may recall, I have been IT Training Manager at County Trust for the past few years, and have experience of this type of large-scale software change-over. The problems that I've successfully handled include:

- slow turn-around rate of departmental change;
- unhelpful training manuals;

- staff resistance to change.

I believe that I could make a significant contribution to Astra at this time, and would welcome the opportunity to discuss this with you further. I will call your office in the next few days to arrange an appointment.

Yours sincerely

Sam Tarrent

Another of Sam's letters to Julian is included in Chapter 13, *Follow-up letters*.

Topical letters prompted by a mutual acquaintance

A colleague of Diane's has told her that Lewis Dean has a vacancy coming up shortly in his department, and might be interested in seeing the sort of work that she does. Rather than waiting for the position to be advertised, Diane has written to him directly.

- Diane uses Alan's name as an introduction and, to some extent, a recommendation.
- As well as her CV, she has included a copy of the campaign that will be of most interest to the company. This is better than asking someone to look through her entire portfolio at this stage.
- She doesn't give many details about herself, focusing on her wide experience instead. Diane intends to let the enclosed example of her work speak for itself.
- If Lewis Dean is interested in what she has shown him so far, he can see the rest of her work at a later meeting.
- Diane emphasises the extremely good results that this particular campaign achieved. This is a very important point

that will not be apparent from the enclosed example. However good the campaign may look, the thing that matters most to a prospective employer is what it accomplished.

- As there is more than one enclosure – her CV and a copy of her campaign – Diane has put 'Encs' rather than 'Enc' below her name.

2 Southerwood Drive
Handley Hill
Edgerton
Devon
EG17 8GH

Tel: 00000 000000

4 May 2008

Mr Lewis Dean
Manager
J J&D Partnership
Hay House
Mandover
Devon
DE8 9PT

Dear Mr Dean

Alan Watts suggested that I contact you concerning a position in your advertising department in which I feel I could make a significant contribution.

As you will see from the enclosed career details, I have worked extensively on a range of accounts including consumer, recruitment, and financial. I have wide experience of creating exciting and imaginative advertising and publicity campaigns.

Of particular interest to you will be my 2007 campaign on behalf of Eurocorp, a copy of which I enclose, which prompted a response rate of 43 per cent, the highest ever achieved by this agency.

I am confident that I could be a valuable addition to your team and would appreciate the opportunity to discuss it further with you. I will ring within the next few days to arrange an appointment.

Yours sincerely

Diane Ashford
Encs

7

Getting started

General points

Whether you are leaving school, college or university, finding your first job isn't easy. You have no work record that employers can refer to, and they have little on which to base their judgement of you.

You need to convince your future employer that you have qualities that will be useful to them in the workplace. Although your academic record may be good, this, surprisingly, is often not what is of most interest to employers. The qualities that they tend to value more are:

- reliability;
- a positive attitude;
- pride in your work;
- the ability to work as part of a team;
- the ability to follow instructions accurately;
- punctuality;
- trustworthiness;
- a willingness to learn;

- enthusiasm;
- accuracy;
- the ability to work with customers or clients;
- initiative;
- friendliness;
- an appropriate appearance;
- the ability to handle problems appropriately.

Your letters should highlight any of these qualities that you have. You could also include some idea of how, when and where you have demonstrated them.

A prospective employer will be interested in any work experience that you have had. It doesn't matter if your experience is different from the sort of work for which you are applying; it will still demonstrate that you are familiar with a working environment. You can show that you appreciate the importance of punctuality, following instructions, being responsible, etc.

Your experience needn't necessarily be in paid employment, either. Include any voluntary work that you may have done, as well as work placements or work experience courses, especially if they are of relevance to the sort of work that you wish to do.

Highlight any special duties or responsibilities that you may have undertaken at school or college. Include anything that rounds out the picture of you as a responsible and dependable individual with experience of more than just the classroom or lecture hall.

One thing that you can definitely bring to the job is enthusiasm. Reflect this in the tone of your letter, along with your interest and motivation.

If possible, try to find common links between your qualifications, your interests and the position for which you are applying. It will be easier for the reader to believe in your enthusiasm and commitment if they can see logical reasons for your interest.

What you need to get across

Include the following points in your letter:

- Any of those desirable qualities that you have, such as reliability, a positive attitude, pride in your work, etc.
- The opportunities that you have had to demonstrate these.
- Any working experience that you have had.
- Any other relevant experience that you have had.
- Any understanding of the job, the company, or of this type of work that you may have.
- Your enthusiasm for this job, or for this company.
- Your qualifications.
- Any other skills that you have.
- Any other points that make you suitable for this particular job.

The school leaver

- Timothy opens with a clear statement of why he is writing.
- He gives a brief account of his schooling and qualifications. Note that he doesn't give all his GCSEs, just the relevant ones. These will usually be Maths and English, and Timothy includes Woodwork as well because the job is in a DIY store.
- He mentions all his work experience, even though none of it is in warehousing. He talks about the garden supply shop first, as this may be somewhat similar to the DIY store. He also mentions that he works as a shelf filler, indicating that he is used to lifting and carrying safely, something he may have to do as a warehouse assistant.

- With this experience, he is able to go on to say that he enjoys being busy and working hard as part of a team. Teamwork is specifically mentioned in the advertisement.
- The advertisement also mentions the necessity for on-the-job training. Timothy shows his enthusiasm and commitment through his willingness to undertake further training. He also shows that he has read the advertisement carefully by mentioning this and the previous point.

43 Hopwood Road
Hopton Kingslade
Nottinghamshire
NH3 3BE

Tel: 00000 000000

4 June 2008

Mr James Erskine
Manager
Digby DIY
Holmwood Lane
Worksop
Nottinghamshire
NH14 6BD

Dear Mr Erskine

I am writing in answer to your advertisement in today's Nottinghamshire *Daily Record* for a trainee warehouse assistant.

I shall be leaving Kingslade Comprehensive School at the end of this month having taken five GCSEs including Maths, English and Woodwork. I have worked every holiday for the past two years at BJ Garden Supplies as a general assistant, and currently work Saturdays at Green Stores supermarket as a shelf filler.

I enjoy being busy and working hard as part of a team. I would especially welcome the chance of on-the-job training.

I have enclosed my CV and look forward to hearing from you.

Yours sincerely

Timothy Gaines
Enc CV

The college leaver

- In this letter, Jane concentrates on her skills and qualifications, as they are highly relevant to the job for which she is applying.
- Note that she explains exactly what the course covers, rather than just giving the course title and hoping that the reader will know what this means. Indirectly this also demonstrates that Jane understands what the job will entail.
- Even though she does not mention any work experience, the tone of her letter comes across as extremely businesslike and efficient. Even the layout indicates her efficient approach; it is possible to take in all the relevant points at a glance.
- She has picked out the key words 'self-motivated and dependable' from the advertisement and used them appropriately.
- Jane has selected her special options carefully to underline a common link between her interests and qualifications and the job for which she is applying.
- She further highlights this link in her use of the phrase 'As you will see from my special options...' The effect of this is to demonstrate enthusiasm and commitment to working in finance.

Ref: 7/TC Administration Assistant
Jane Clark [jclarke@anyisp.co.uk]
To: tcrispin@benn-hodge-keen.com

Dear Mr Crispin

I wish to apply for the above position as advertised on jobs.com.

I am currently attending a one-year Business Administration course at the local College of Further Education, having already successfully completed RSA Typing Stage I. The topics covered in the course include:

- office administration;
- communication skills;
- information technology;
- data processing;
- business correspondence.

I am also taking further special options in:

- financial administration;
- business finance;
- spreadsheets.

I am self-motivated and dependable, and I look forward to developing a career in office administration. As you will see from my special options, I would be particularly interested in joining a financial agency such as yourselves.

I am available for interview at any time and look forward to hearing from you.

Yours sincerely

Jane Clark
33 West Road
Long Ashley
East Sussex
BT17 8RJ

jclark@anyisp.co.uk

Tel: 00000 000000

The graduate

- Ellen is applying for a position as Project Assistant for a health care project aimed at finding out what sort of help and information would be useful to new mothers.
- By mentioning that she saw the advertisement on the local health authority's website, Ellen shows that she is interested enough in her field to keep up with current events.
- She briefly outlines her academic qualifications, which are in line with those required for the post.
- The major part of her letter centres on her greatest strength: her first-hand, practical experience of working with the public in health care.
- Although she has no experience of paid employment, Ellen has plenty of highly relevant experience through work placement and voluntary work. She explains this experience fully, and uses it to highlight her suitability for this position.
- She manages to get across abilities such as working with people, communicating effectively, plus her organisational and administrative skills.
- She underlines her experience in such key areas as working in preventive health, working with women, working in hospital, etc.
- Taking up a voluntary job indicates her initiative and commitment. This also communicates her interest, enthusiasm and motivation. She effectively links up her qualifications and interests with the position for which she is applying.

21 College Place
Crossley
Wilts
WT6 6GG

Tel: 00000 000000
e-mail: esharp@anyisp.com

20 May 2008

Mrs Linda French
Project Director
Deerfield Health Authority
PO Box 20
Deerfield
Oxon
OX44 9BN

Dear Mrs French

I have recently completed my degree in Health Studies at the South of England University and I would like to apply for the position of Project Assistant currently advertised on your website.

My undergraduate courses included Health Sciences and Social Psychology, and I also completed supplementary courses on Information Technology and Data Handling. Full details of these are included in my enclosed CV.

My work experience to date includes a three-month work placement at the Littlemead Centre as part of the health awareness scheme there. I very much enjoyed the experience of working with the public, and found the project both stimulating and rewarding. I was able to communicate effectively on all levels, and I discovered an enthusiasm for organisation, and a commitment to preventive health care. This, in turn, led to my being involved, as a voluntary worker, with the foundation of the Women's Health Unit at Southcross Hospital.

I would be very interested to learn more about your own project and I look forward to hearing from you in the near future.

Yours sincerely

Ellen Sharp
Enc CV

The school leaver: a speculative letter

- Amanda is sending out speculative letters to companies that might have an opening for a school leaver. This is a standard letter that Amanda will copy and send out many times. But, even though she is sending letters to a number of organisations, she still sends each one to a named individual.
- She has also included a personal touch by mentioning G&C's reputation for training and development. This shows that she has researched the company and knows something about them.
- She gives a clear idea of the sort of work that interests her, but leaves the details fairly open at this stage.
- Her request for a trainee vacancy, and her mention of G&C's training programme, indicate that she is keen to get ahead and is well motivated.
- Amanda talks about her work experience and relates it to the qualities that she knows employers will appreciate. This also demonstrates that she has a clear idea of what they will expect from her in work: punctuality, dependability, accuracy and initiative.
- Like Timothy, she mentions how many GCSEs she is taking, and gives the most relevant ones, but doesn't give the whole list.
- She makes a logical link between one of her GCSE subjects and the type of job she is looking for.
- As this is a speculative letter, she closes by asking them to keep her on file for future reference. If Amanda hasn't heard from them in six months, and she is still looking for a job, she will send them an updated letter.

For more information about this type of letter, see Chapter 6, *Speculative letters*.

33 Sherbourne Crescent
Trent East
South Yorkshire
YS17 8PP

Tel: 00000 000000

11 June 2008

Ms Kay Davies
Personnel Manager
G&C Ltd
Tower Dean
South Yorkshire
YS10 8AS

Dear Ms Davies

I am writing to enquire if you have any trainee vacancies in your company. I am 16 years old and I will be leaving Bradenfield Comprehensive at the end of this year, having completed five GCSEs including Maths, English and Computer Studies.

I am particularly interested in keyboard work, either word-processing or data entry, and I understand that G&C has a very good reputation for training and development in both these areas.

I am hard-working and dependable, with a good eye for detail, and work well both on my own and in a team. My work at a local shop at the weekends and during the holidays has taught me the value of punctuality and to follow instructions accurately. It has also given me confidence in my ability to handle day-to-day problems appropriately.

I am available for interview at any time, and I look forward to hearing from you with any information or advice that you might have. Should you not be recruiting currently, I would greatly appreciate your keeping my name on file for the future.

Yours sincerely

Amanda Riddle

The college leaver: a speculative letter

- Francis is sending speculative letters to all the companies that might be interested in someone with his qualifications. This is a standard letter that he will copy and send out many times. But even though he is sending letters to a number of organisations, he still sends each one to a named individual.
- Francis gives a clear idea of the sort of work that interests him, but is not specific at this stage. To some extent, as with most graduates, his qualifications will dictate his job options.
- His academic qualifications are fairly standard and will be shared by many others applying for jobs, so Francis concentrates attention on one of his stronger points – his work experience.
- Although he has no experience of paid work, he has plenty of relevant experience from a holiday placement. Frances relates this experience to the qualities generally appreciated by employers. He links what he has done to the type of industrial work done by the company.
- He underlines his enthusiasm for this type of work.
- In closing, he emphasises his keenness by requesting a meeting, and includes a request for help and advice.

For more information about this type of letter, see Chapter 6, *Speculative letters*.

4 Aspen Terrace
West Kiddington
Worcester
WT7 7JT

Tel: 00000 000000
e-mail: frandearley@anyisp.com

3 May 2008

Mr Simon Aylsham
Head: Industrial Division
Apton Chemicals
Coburg Industrial Estate
Stafford
SF17 9HH

Dear Mr Aylsham

I will be completing a BSc Degree in Chemistry this autumn and I am writing to you to enquire whether you would have a suitable vacancy for a newly qualified industrial chemist.

My undergraduate courses included both organic and inorganic chemistry, and I also completed supplementary courses in mathematics and computing.

My work experience to date includes a summer placement with Harper's Industrial Division, assisting on alkali-wash trials for the treatment of petroleum waste. I very much enjoyed working in an industrial laboratory, and found the experience both interesting and rewarding. I learned how to operate as part of a team and to communicate effectively at all levels. During my time there, I also discovered an aptitude for detailed and accurate work. Full information on the duties undertaken is included in my enclosed CV.

Should you not be recruiting currently, I would greatly appreciate your keeping my name on file for future reference. I would, in any case, be very interested in a short meeting with you to discuss possible career prospects in your field. I will contact your office shortly to request a convenient time and date.

Yours sincerely

Francis Dearley
Enc CV

8

Starting again

General points

At some time in your life, you may find yourself re-entering the job market after a break. This can be for a number of reasons, the most usual being after:

- bringing up a family;
- a period of unemployment;
- an accident or illness.

The problems that you face on re-entering the market are similar to those facing someone going into it for the first time: you need to convince prospective employers that you are 'job-ready' and will fit into the working environment. You will need to convey to them that you still understand the qualities that employers require, such as dependability, punctuality, the ability to handle problems – and that you are capable of displaying these qualities. In addition, employers sometimes anticipate problems that relate to your specific situation as a returner, and you need to address these concerns in your letter.

Depending on how long you have been out of employment, things may have changed a lot since you were last in work. An employer may worry about whether you are up to date with what's happening in your industry. They may also wonder if you would be willing to adapt to new ways of doing things, or if you would stick to the ways that you already know.

Make sure your letter shows you as someone who is lively and well motivated, with a clear sense of purpose. Show that you have kept in step with business in general, and your field in particular. Your career break may have been accidental, or you may have taken it for excellent reasons, but your future employer is chiefly interested in knowing that you have a commitment to working now.

Don't apologise for your career break; mention it briefly in a business-like manner, and move on to discuss your positive qualities. Gaps in employment, for whatever reason, are a fact of life, and can be handled positively and assertively.

Underline your enthusiasm for the job and the organisation. Show your motivation and commitment to getting back into work in the tone of your letter. Make it clear, though, that you are enthusiastic about *this* job, rather than just *any* job. Say what it is that particularly appeals to you about it, and in what way you are particularly suited to it.

As in all application letters, emphasise your relevant experience, and concentrate on the skills and qualities that you can bring to this vacancy. Draw people's attention to what you *have* done, rather than what you haven't.

Project confidence and self-assurance in what you write, but balance your certainty that you can do the job with a clear willingness to learn and adapt. Point out, where possible, how you have kept up your skills during this break, and mention anything that you have done to improve or update them. Any training you have done during this time will be a useful indicator of your interest and motivation, and should be included. It's not a bad idea, in any case, to aim to go back to the workplace better qualified than when you left it.

It may be that you want to change your line of work after this break. If so, try to connect the three parts of your working life: your previous employment, your experience during the break, and your chosen future employment. Do this in a way that would make sense to anyone reading your letter.

Read Chapter 5, *Answering advertised vacancies,* for more general information on application letters, and Chapter 6, *Speculative letters,* if you are thinking of sending off any of these. Chapter 10, *Troubleshooting,* may also be helpful.

What you need to get across

Think about including the following points:

- Any and all work experience that you have had during your career break, including voluntary work, part-time work, special responsibilities and duties, etc.
- Your positive attitude towards continuing your work.
- Your commitment and enthusiasm.
- The way in which this job fits in with your intended career pattern.
- Your achievements to date.
- Any training that you have undertaken during your break, or any other way in which you have kept up your skills.
- The way in which you have kept abreast of developments in your trade or profession.
- The answers to any specific worries that you can anticipate. A statement about your current guaranteed good health if you have had a break due to illness, for example.
- Positive ways in which you have changed – increased maturity, for example, or more responsibility, confidence, understanding, new skills, insight, etc.

The woman returner – 1

- In the following letter, Anne concentrates on her strengths – her qualifications and her wide range of experience.
- The whole tone of her letter is businesslike and competent, emphasising her probable skills in this area.
- She gives details of her last job, emphasising the opportunities for professional growth and development. This suggests that she has a commitment to continuing her career, and sees this current vacancy as part of a wider career structure.
- Anne briefly states that she left her last position to look after her child, but also mentions that she was with the company for three years before leaving. This suggests her commitment and stability.
- She tells them what she has done during her four-year career break, and emphasises her continued interest in her field of work. None of the courses she has done has been particularly demanding or time-consuming, but they have broadened her outlook and raised her general level of competence.
- She makes it clear that she is better qualified and better trained now than when she left her previous job.
- In her closing paragraph, Anne summarises her skills and what she has to offer. She does this with the original job advertisement in mind, which asks for particular qualities such as experience and the ability to tackle problems.
- She clearly states that she is now ready to return to work, and outlines the sort of job and organisation for which she is looking. These, of course, are broadly in line with those of the advertised vacancy.

2 Holm Place
Jessop
Leicester
LE1 9KK

Tel: 0000 000 0000

5 February 2009

Ms Diane Hughes
Personnel Director
Apted International Ltd
PO Box 9
Leicester
LE12 6DV

Dear Ms Hughes

<u>Re: Position of Personnel Officer, Reference S17/PO</u>

I wish to apply for the position of Personnel Officer as advertised in the *North Leicester Record* on 5 February 2009.

As you will see from my enclosed CV, I left the Business School of Borough College of Higher Education with a BTEC National Diploma in Personnel Management. Since then I have gained a wide variety of experience in a number of different posts, both full and part time.

My work in such diverse industries as engineering, retail and pharmaceuticals has, I believe, allowed me to develop skill and confidence in dealing with a wide range of people and workplace problems.

My most recent position was with Harper Daniels, where I was Staff Liaison Officer, a satisfying and challenging post that offered much opportunity for professional growth and development. I was with them for three years until 2005, when I left to take up full-time child-care.

During this time I successfully completed a course in Basic Counselling. I have also taken the opportunity to revise my basic personnel competencies through a series of short courses run by the Institute of Personnel Administration.

I believe I am well suited to the position offered. I am experienced and competent with a good track record in interpersonal skills and problem-solving. I am now seeking to return to a full-time career position in a large, forward-thinking company that offers excellent employment opportunities.

I am available for interview at any time and I look forward to hearing from you.

Yours sincerely

Anne Timmins
Enc CV

The woman returner – 2

- Lucy's letter concentrates on her biggest achievements at her previous job: the emergency training of administrative staff, and the successful introduction of an apprentice training scheme.
- The company she is applying to also has an apprentice scheme, and this aspect of her previous job will interest them.
- Note that she doesn't draw attention to the fact that she has only worked for one company since leaving college. Instead, she draws the reader's attention to what she has done, rather than what she hasn't.
- The tone of her letter is warmer and more approachable than Anne's, giving the picture of a different sort of person with, probably, a different approach to the job. It is interesting to note how personality can come over even in business letters.
- She states that she left her last position to look after her children, but also mentions that she found her work varied

and stimulating. This suggests that she is looking forward to returning to employment.

- She emphasises what she has gained from her experience of child-rearing, and how this relates to the job for which she is applying.
- She makes it clear that she has improved her key qualities since leaving her previous job.
- In her closing paragraph, Lucy summarises her skills and what she has to offer. She does this bearing in mind the original job advertisement, which asks for particular qualities such as flexibility and the ability to enjoy challenges.
- She clearly states that she is looking forward to returning to work, and outlines the sort of organisation for which she is looking. This, of course, is broadly in line with the description of the company placing the advertisement.

43 Rosemead
Stanhope
Cumbria
CU7 1MB

Tel: 00000 000000

3 February 2009

Miss Vera Stanstead
Training Director
NNG Aero-Engineering Ltd
PO Box 99
CU99 4RV

Dear Miss Stanstead

I wish to apply for the post of Training and Assessment Officer advertised in this week's *Vacancies Bulletin.*

As you will see from my enclosed CV, I was employed at Humberland Ltd as a Training and Development Officer, having gained City & Guilds 3901 Trainer's Competency from

Landston College. My major achievements in this position include the full training of over 40 administrative staff in less than three months. This was during the introduction of a new data-processing system. In addition, I was also responsible for the introduction of a complete 'Quality First' apprentice module that increased apprentice productivity by 15 per cent.

I left Humberland Ltd in 2004 after six varied and stimulating years in order to bring up my two children full time. The experience of child-care has, I believe, developed my skills of patience and organisation, as well as further strengthening my aptitude for effective communication.

I am looking forward to resuming my career. I am a flexible, hard-working, professional trainer who enjoys the challenge of working for a large, progressive organisation such as yourselves. I would welcome the opportunity to discuss the position with you more fully and look forward to hearing from you in the near future.

Yours sincerely

Lucy Keel
Enc CV

Returning after a period of unemployment – 1

- Patrick concentrates on his suitability for the post on offer. His opening paragraph is almost a direct rephrasing of the advertisement put into his own words.
- He chooses to direct the reader to his CV rather than include details of his achievements in his letter. He summarises by saying that he is 'a successful sales executive of many years' experience'. His CV contains details of all the achievements that back up this statement.
- The tone of the letter is competent and assured, without sounding too boastful.

- He gives details of his last job, emphasising the opportunities for professional growth and development. This suggests that he has a commitment to his career, and sees this current vacancy as part of longer-term developments.
- Patrick briefly states that he left his last position because of redundancy, but emphasises that it was the *job* that became redundant, not him. He also briefly summarises the background to this event.
- He gives great emphasis to what he has been doing during his enforced break. He has updated and upgraded his skills and qualities considerably during this time. He has also shown his drive and initiative in setting up and running a presentation skills course voluntarily.
- He clearly states, however, that it is a full-time career position that he seeks, and outlines the sort of company for which he is looking. This, of course, is broadly similar to the one that advertised the vacancy.
- In his closing paragraph, Patrick repeats his belief in his suitability for the job and his conviction that he has much to offer.

23 August 2008

Mr Mark Reed
Sales Director
Dandy Ltd
Redding Road
North Lea
Norfolk
NR16 1DX

Dear Mr Reed

I wish to apply for the post of Area Sales Manager advertised in today's *Advertiser.*

I believe I am well suited to the position offered. As you will see from my enclosed CV, I am a successful sales executive of many years' experience. I am looking for a position where I can put my competence and integrity to good use and achieve major business goals.

My most recent position was with J&H Ridings, where I was Senior Sales Associate, a satisfying and challenging post that offered much opportunity for professional growth and development. I was with them until earlier this year when, due to the merger of J&H Ridings with Bern Uttoxeter, my position was made redundant.

I am at present completing a course in Communication Skills. In addition, I have taken this opportunity to consolidate and update my sales and marketing techniques through a series of one-day seminars run by the University Business School. I am also running, in a voluntary capacity, a short course on presentation skills at my local Job Club. I now seek to return to a permanent, full-time career position in a company that offers first-rate opportunities for development.

I am confident that I would make a valuable contribution to Dandy Ltd, and would welcome the opportunity to discuss this further. I look forward to hearing from you.

Yours sincerely

Patrick Lowe
Enc CV

Returning after a period of unemployment – 2

- Donald uses his recent experience of working as a warehouse supervisor to support his application for the job of Stock Records Clerk.
- Note that he doesn't say initially that his current work is voluntary. The job carries a full range of duties and responsibilities, and it has broadened Donald's experience. The only difference between this and a 'proper' job is that Donald doesn't get paid for it. He, accordingly, gives it its full value in his letter and in his CV.
- Throughout his letter, Donald includes the skills and qualities that Dutch Industrial have asked for in their advertisement, putting them into his own words as he does so.

- He briefly mentions that he is looking for a new job as the result of large-scale redundancy, and gives some background to the event.
- He quickly goes on to concentrate the reader's attention on what he has been doing since. He puts this in very positive terms, and his enthusiasm comes across in the letter.
- The whole tone of the letter is vigorous, approachable and enthusiastic, without being in any way 'gushing'.
- He closes by saying that he wants to return to permanent, full-time work, and specifically mentioning the company's name.
- Note that if you say in your letter that you want to work for a specific company, you must do your homework before the interview. One of the first questions they are likely to ask is *why* you want to work for them.

5 March 2009

Mr E J Fenn
Personnel Manager
Dutch Industrial
Unit 7
Impney Industrial Estate
Impney
Hertfordshire
HE19 9BV

Dear Mr Fenn

Re: Stock Records Clerk, Reference Vac/SR3/Het

I wish to apply for the position of Stock Records Clerk as advertised in the *Kingsdean Mercury* today, 5 March 2009.

My experience as Stock Control Clerk at Norwich International, plus my recent position as Warehouse Supervisor for National Charities leaves me, I believe, well qualified for the post.

I am reliable and competent, and very good at handling a variety of tasks efficiently and responsibly. I mix well with others and am used to working co-operatively as part of a team.

As you will see from the enclosed CV, my most recent position was with Myers Fabrications. Sadly, the company closed at the end of last year, making many of my colleagues and myself redundant. Since then I have put my skills and experience to good use in the community. I have been working at the National Charities regional depot, ensuring the efficient distribution of both donated items and fund-raising goods. This project was both interesting and challenging, but I am now looking for a permanent full-time position with a large commercial company such as Dutch Industrial.

I am available for interview at any time, and look forward to hearing from you.

Yours sincerely

Donald Rice
Enc CV

Returning after illness

- Catherine has been very unlucky. She was involved in a bad accident that meant she had to take nearly a year off to recover. Not knowing how long it would be before she could work again, the company she worked for couldn't keep her job open.
- In her letter, Catherine concentrates on her skills and qualifications, and underlines the two key skills that they have specifically asked for that she can supply: fluent commercial French, and familiarity with spreadsheets.
- Note that she says she is 'familiar with handling business spreadsheets'. This means exactly what it says – she

understands what they are, and has used them in the past. They are not asking for someone who is a specialist.

- The tone of her letter is calm, serious and considered. She sums herself up as 'a professional secretary'. This is appropriate to the type of job for which she is applying, and also echoes the style of the company to which she is applying – a long-established, top-rank finance house.
- She emphasises her familiarity with the type of work that she would be doing, and the similarity to previous jobs that she has done. She deliberately picks up key points from her CV, such as her job with 'a fellow finance house'. The implication is that she will pick up this new job quickly, and fit in easily.
- She mentions her accident in order to explain why she is now looking for work. Having done so, she quickly goes on to say that she has now fully recovered and is looking forward to getting back to work.
- She focuses attention on the positive things that she has been doing since her accident: upgrading and updating her word-processing skills. This not only emphasises her interest and motivation for her work, but also underlines that she is now fit and well. If she is strong enough to take a course, she is probably well enough to start work again without any problems.

21 July 2008

Mrs Ann Clarke
Office Manager
Curtiss Financial Ltd
Aston Buildings
London
EC4 4UH

Dear Mrs Clarke

I would like to apply for the position of Department Secretary advertised in today's edition of the *Chronicle.*

As your advertisement requests, I am fluent in commercial French and familiar with handling business spreadsheets.

You will see from my enclosed career details that, since successfully completing the Westmoor College bilingual secretarial course, I have had extensive office and secretarial experience. This includes three years with Litman Holdings, a fellow finance house, and a year with Morrisot International, six months of which were spent at their Paris branch.

I am a professional secretary – patient, calm under pressure, and resourceful. My work is proficient and accurate, and I aim for the highest standards of presentation.

My most recent position was with Miller & Hills, legal consultants. Regrettably, a long stay in hospital following a car accident some months ago meant that I was no longer able to continue with them. I have now, however, fully recovered and look forward to resuming my career. I have used my convalescence to good effect by upgrading my computer skills at the local training centre with the addition of Microsoft PowerPoint.

I would be most happy to discuss my application with you further, and I am currently available for interview at any time.

Yours sincerely

Catherine Holden
Enc CV

9

Carrying on

General points

At some stage in your life, you may find yourself in the position of wanting to carry on your career in changed circumstances. This can be for a number of reasons, but the most common are:

- after retirement;
- during education or training;
- while bringing up children;
- after discharge from the Services;
- after relocation.

Because of your altered circumstances, you may find that you are applying for jobs that are quite different from the sort of work that you have done in the past. You may decide that it suits you better to apply for part-time work. Or you may wish to apply for jobs that could be seen as 'inferior', in terms of pay, duties or responsibilities, to the sort of work you are used to doing.

In each case, you need to make your reasons for taking such a step logical and reasonable. Help the reader to understand what you are trying to achieve, and where this particular position fits in.

Relate this current vacancy to your previous experience as much as possible. Show how the skills and qualities you have developed will be of value to your prospective employer.

What you need to get across

Consider the following points for inclusion in your letter.

- How this job fits into your overall career pattern.
- Your reasons for wanting to do this job.
- The way in which you fit this position.
- The relevant skills and qualities you can bring to the vacancy.
- Your enthusiasm and commitment for the job. Make sure your prospective employer knows that you are not regarding this as a temporary stop-gap until something better comes along.

After retirement

- Edward has taken early retirement. He feels that this would be a good time to change the sort of work that he does.
- He opens the main part of his letter with his reasons for applying for this job, rather than looking for the sort of job he used to do.
- He mentions his engineering skills and experience. They will be useful in this job, especially his breadth of experience.
- Edward relates the specific skills that he has used in developing his staff, and working with trainees, to the skills that he will need for this job.
- He also ties in his other interest in the local boys' club. Even though this is not part of his paid employment, it is relevant to his application.

- He gives a brief sketch of his character – outgoing and down-to-earth. This is appropriate for the sort of work that he hopes to be doing, and also fits in with the style of the organisation that placed the advertisement.
- Overall, Edward presents a logical and convincing application. By selecting relevant skills and experience, he ties together what he has done in the past with what he intends to do in the future.

1 The Dingles
Coveringham
Lincoln
LN17 6QZ

Tel: 00000 000000
e-mail: edlong@anyisp.com

19 September 2008

Mr Philip Turner
Co-ordinator
The Apprentice Project
The Frean Centre
Lincoln LN4 7HH

Dear Mr Turner

<u>Re: Supervisor, Engineering Training Unit</u>

I am writing to apply for the above position as advertised in the Coveringham *Community Bulletin.*

I am an engineer of many years' experience and, having taken early retirement in June of this year, I am now keen to use my skills for the benefit of the wider community.

As you will see from my enclosed CV, I have an extensive background in engineering and have, during my 30 years in the industry, encountered and solved many problems, both with machines and with people. I have, in that time, also identified and developed the potential of many of my staff.

I feel confident that my knowledge and expertise can be of value in the position you offer.

In addition to practical engineering skills, I also have many years of experience with apprentices and trainees in the workplace, and I have, for the past 10 years, been actively involved with my local boys' club. I find working with young people immensely rewarding and well worth the time and energy invested.

I am an outgoing, down-to-earth person who enjoys being involved with whatever is going on. I believe I have both the background and the character to make an important contribution to your scheme.

I would very much enjoy hearing more about the workshop and am available for interview at any time. I look forward to hearing from you.

Yours sincerely

Edward Longley
Enc CV

Part-time work – 1

- Leigh is doing a part-time college course, and is interested in getting some practical experience as well as earning some extra money.
- She opens her letter with her reasons for applying for a part-time job, rather than looking for a full-time one. She presents these reasons in a very positive way, seeing it as an opportunity to complement her studies.
- She mentions her previous skills and experience that are relevant to the job for which she is currently applying.
- Leigh suggests that she might be a good long-term investment for Croft & Croft, as well as fulfilling their short-term requirements. If they employ her now, at the end

of her course they will have someone well trained in information technology. They will also have someone who knows the company well, and understands what they want and need.

- With this in mind, she gives a brief outline of the skills she will be acquiring on the course.
- She comes across as keen and motivated, with plenty of initiative.

29 September 2008

Mrs Sandra Ellis
Personnel Manager
Croft & Croft
East Coats
North Yorkshire
YS2 2IS

Dear Mrs Ellis

I am writing to apply for the position of part-time data administration clerk advertised in today's *Bisleigh Herald.*

Having recently started a two-year part-time Information Technology Course at Coats College, I am interested in the opportunity that this position offers to complement my studies with real experience.

As you will see from my enclosed CV, I already have a sound background in office skills, having spent three years with Arthur J Long as a clerk. When I decided to return to college this autumn, it was with a view to continuing training, expanding and updating these skills in line with the requirements of the modern office. I believe that what I am currently learning would be of value to Croft & Croft both in the short term and in the long term. Briefly this includes:

- office automation;
- business technology;
- data handling;

- computer skills:
  - Word;
  - Access;
  - Excel;
  - Outlook.

I would welcome the opportunity to discuss my application further with you and look forward to hearing from you in the near future.

Yours sincerely

Leigh Scott
Enc CV

Part-time work – 2

- Carole opens the main part of her letter with her greatest strength: her thorough experience of this type of work.
- She goes on to state her special skill – she speaks fluent German – which the advertisement specifically asked for.
- Carole describes herself using key phrases from the advertisement and putting them in her own words.
- She goes on to tell them about her main achievements in her previous jobs. Someone who is going to save them time, and improve productivity, will be of interest to most companies.
- By this stage, the reader is probably wondering why Carole is looking for part-time work. Her reason is in the closing paragraph.
- Carole puts her reasons clearly, and sounds positive, enthusiastic and motivated. Wanting to combine work with home commitments will make sense to a prospective employer.

49 Challenger Road
Whitpool
Kent
KT4 1AA

Tel: 00000 000000

3 April 2009

Mr F C Glynn
Director
Quay Import & Export
Bishop's Way
Dover
KN7 9OL

Dear Mr Glynn

I am writing to apply for the position of part-time Import Administrator advertised in this week's *Journal*.

I have thorough experience of this type of work, including two years with Russell Exports as Export Supervisor at their Dover site, and three years at Gold Trading as an import clerk. I am, in addition, bilingual, with fluent business German gained from an 18-month secondment to the Munich branch of Crafthouse Processing.

I am self-motivated, conscientious and hard-working, with the ability to work both independently and as a co-operative team member. My greatest achievements to date include cutting the invoice turnaround time at Russell Exports by 15 per cent, and the introduction of a new docketing system that improved the speed of processing by 10 per cent.

As the mother of two school-age children, I am now looking forward to taking up my career again. I am, therefore, very interested in the opportunity that this position offers to combine my career with my commitments at home.

I look forward to hearing from you in the near future.

Yours sincerely

Carole Hinde

Ex-services

- Robert is retiring from the Navy, having reached the rank of Commander.
- He has spent the majority of his time in the Service working in personnel, and wishes to continue with this line of work in civilian life.
- The opening sentence of the main part of his letter states why he is now looking for a job – he is leaving the Navy.
- He goes on to explain, in a fair amount of detail, the sort of work that he did.
- He needs to emphasise his specific experience in personnel work the way he does because it is not immediately apparent from his previous job title what his duties were.
- His interests – professional development and training – are in line with the requirements stated in the job advertisement, so they are worth mentioning specifically in this way.
- He puts in a word about Erskine & Dunne that is flattering without sounding too gushing.
- Robert is also interested in his own development and training. He mentions that he has IPD qualifications, and emphasises that he wishes to continue his studies. This means that he will probably become even more valuable to the company as time goes by.
- He closes on a confident note. Indeed, the tone of the letter overall is confident and businesslike.

Flat 4, 33 Broad Way
Devonport
Devon
DV2 7FF

Tel: 00000 000000

21 May 2009

Mr E J Klein
Senior Personnel Officer
Erskine & Dunne
Lower Place Road
Lincoln
LN3 6GV

Dear Mr Klein

Re: Personnel Manager

Please find enclosed my CV in application for the above position as advertised in the *National Gazette* on Thursday, 18 May 2009.

I have just completed seven years in the Navy, achieving the rank of Commander. During this time I worked primarily in personnel management, and had full responsibility for the recruitment and training of all personnel, both military and civilian. I believe that my experience has given me the qualifications and background to undertake the duties of this post.

My interests have focused on the areas of professional development and training, and I would welcome the opportunity to develop these areas further within a company with the reputation of Erskine & Dunne. I also hope to continue my own studies and achieve my IPD Fellowship in the near future.

I am confident that I could make a valuable contribution in the position advertised, and I would welcome further discussion of my application. I look forward to hearing from you.

Yours sincerely

Robert Fisher
Enc CV

Moving to a new area

- Amelia is continuing her career after moving from another part of the country.
- Her first main paragraph tells the reader about her last position.
- She draws clear parallels between the skills and qualities required in her last job, and those specifically requested in the advertisement for this job.
- At the end of this paragraph, she explains why she had to leave Bellgate – her husband's relocation due to promotion.
- She also says how much she enjoyed working for them, which indicates that she will enjoy working for a similar company.
- The advertisement specifically mentions the word 'challenge' and Amelia, again, uses this to reflect the attitude that Danby & Watson require.
- She starts her second paragraph confidently and positively, and goes on to mention her NVQ. This highlights her enthusiasm for her work, and initiative in undertaking further training.
- Amelia then outlines her main achievement with Bellgate. Most organisations will be interested in someone who is capable of improving department efficiency.

27 The Paddock
Gilby
Stourling
HU12 1DD

Tel: 00000 000000

5 March 2009

Ms Wendy Carpenter
Personnel Officer
Danby & Watson Manufacturing
Danesgate
Holmby
HU7 5PO

Dear Ms Carpenter

I am writing in reply to your advertisement in today's *Evening Echo* requesting applications for the post of Senior Secretary to the Productivity Department.

My most recent position was as Personal Assistant to the Director of Bellgate Industrial. I found this job used my aptitude for working on my own initiative as well as providing the opportunity for developing my administrative skills. Although I very much enjoyed the challenge of working for Bellgate, I had to leave them earlier this year when my husband was promoted and we moved to this part of the country.

I am now eager to continue my career, and believe that I have the qualifications and experience required for this position. I have recently completed an NVQ level 2 in Administration, and feel confident that I could make an immediate contribution to the department. My achievements at Bellgate included the successful development of their computerised filing system, which improved office efficiency considerably and substantially decreased resource wastage. Further details are in the enclosed CV.

Thank you for considering my application, I look forward to hearing from you in the near future.

Yours sincerely

Amelia Richie
Enc CV

Troubleshooting

General points

Sometimes, you know in advance that you have a problem applying for a job. This can be a problem that has often arisen, such as being considered too young or too old, or it can be a problem specific to that particular job. Maybe you don't have quite the same qualifications as the ones they are asking for, or your experience is not what they would be anticipating.

It is still worth applying if:

- you have the skills and qualities that are right for the job, even if these are not conventionally expressed;
- you have more skills, qualifications and experience than they are looking for;
- you have the key skills or qualities that they are asking for, but are lacking one of the minor ones;
- you have used some key skills and experience in previous jobs, but need to include other interests to supply the rest;
- you have the right skills and experience, even though you didn't acquire them in paid employment;

- you have the majority of the skills requested, and are in the process of acquiring the rest;
- you have a wealth of experience, but lack formal qualifications;
- you have the experience, and are in the process of acquiring the formal qualifications to back it up.

Adopt an analytical approach. Before you write, put yourself in the employer's position and think about why there might be a problem. Why does your prospective employer, rightly or wrongly, believe that your age, experience, or whatever, will be a difficulty for them? What is it about the job that requires these specific qualities? When you can answer these questions, you can make sure that you cover them adequately in your letter. By anticipating what the reader may be thinking, you can highlight your strongest points, and emphasise those that answer the reader's doubts.

Sometimes anticipated problems are based on stereotypes. You can do a lot to correct the impression that you may give by being, say, under 20 or over 50, by adjusting the tone of your letter and carefully selecting the information that you include.

If you are coming from a very different background, one of their worries might be whether you will fit in. Try to assess the style and tone of the organisation from the way they present themselves, and aim to match this in the presentation of your letter and CV. Use key words where you understand them, but don't include industry jargon unless you are absolutely sure of its meaning and usage.

Try to put things in their terms. The easier it is for the reader to understand what you are telling them, the more likely they are to be sympathetic to your application. Explain your qualifications or experience and give some idea of what each means in practical terms so that the reader has the clearest possible picture of you and your qualities.

Above all, it is very important to emphasise all the points where you match their requirements, rather than dwelling on those areas where you don't. Include any back-up information that will help you to reassure them that you are the right person for the job. Give them all the information you can that will help them to form a favourable opinion of you.

It may also be appropriate to give some idea of why you are applying for this vacancy, even though you may be somewhat at a disadvantage compared to other candidates. You may be able to put a strong case for yourself by showing how this job fits with your past experience and future ambitions. You may also be able to demonstrate a high degree of commitment and enthusiasm for the position.

What you need to get across

Think about including the following points in your letter:

- your strongest points;
- all the things that contradict any preconceived ideas or fears the reader may have;
- all the points that match what they are looking for;
- all the skills, qualities, qualifications and experience that make you suitable for the job;
- what these mean in terms of actual duties and responsibilities;
- how you will fit in with the organisation;
- your reasons for applying for this vacancy;
- any positive qualities that you can bring to the job that are special to you – for example, you may be younger than they require, but you can bring enthusiasm, flexibility, and a willingness to learn.

The older applicant (over 45)

- When an applicant is, like John, over the age of 45, you might anticipate that an employer would worry that:

- his skills aren't up to date;
- he is too set in his ways – he'll find it hard to adapt to a new company;
- he'll resent being told what to do, perhaps by younger people;
- he'll be slow.

John answers many of these worries in his e-mail.

- Although he doesn't state his age, it will be clear from his CV.
- The tone of his letter is confident and energetic, giving a good impression of his character.
- He brings in his major achievement with his current employer early in the letter. A reduction in production costs will interest most companies.
- The achievement he chooses subtly underlines his familiarity and competence with new technology, as well as indicating the level of responsibility that he could bring to the job.
- The letter also underlines that his achievements are recent, not many years in the past.
- He uses active, vigorous words like *challenge, opportunity, pioneering, dynamic.* These give an energetic tone without trying to sound too youthful. He has also mined the job description for important key words.
- He gives a logical and understandable reason for looking for another job at this time. He sounds positive about finding another, similar organisation to work for, and emphasises that he will be continuing, rather than winding down, his career.
- He takes care to mention that his present company value him enough to offer him a job at the new site even though he is unwilling to take up their offer.

- He shows his initiative by undertaking further training to keep his skills up to date and broaden his understanding. He also indicates that he appreciates that keeping up with developments is important. This answers any concerns the reader might have that he thinks 'he knows it all' already.

A303/AJB Industrial Production Engineer
John Lynne [jlynne@anyisp.co.uk]
To: ajbillings@lakestuart.com

Dear Mr Billings

I am contacting you to apply for the above position currently posted on Engineering Online.

As a fully qualified professional engineer with a comprehensive background in industrial production, I believe I fit the requirements stated in your advertisement very well.

I am currently employed by Mono Engineering. My most recent achievement with them has been to play a key role in the installation of the pioneering Formoss production system as part of a cost-cutting exercise earlier this year. To date, the system has resulted in a 10 per cent reduction of production costs.

I have greatly enjoyed my time with Mono; they have provided challenge and the opportunity to develop along with their growth into new markets. Sadly, however, the company will be moving its operations to northern France over the next two years. Although they have offered a placement on the new site, I feel that family commitments oblige me to remain in this country if possible. Consequently, I am looking for a similar dynamic organisation with which to continue my career.

As you will note from the CV that follows, I have recently been updating my technical skills at Redford University with an advanced Computer Assisted Design and Manufacturing (CAD/CAM) course arranged by the Industrial Institute. I have attended many of their courses and seminars and find them an excellent way of keeping up with new developments in the industry.

I should be very pleased to discuss any points with you further, and look forward to hearing from you shortly.

Yours sincerely

John Lynne
Tel: 00000 000000

The younger applicant (under 25)

- With a candidate who is, like Robert, under 25, a prospective employer might be worried that:
  - he doesn't have sufficient experience;
  - he lacks responsibility and dependability;
  - he is under- or over-confident;
  - his communication skills might not be fully developed, and he may have difficulty getting on with people.

Robert has answered these points in his letter.

- Robert doesn't draw attention to his age in his letter, but it will be apparent from his CV how old he is.
- He lets his positive qualities, his skills and experience, speak for him, rather than emphasising his one drawback.
- The tone of his letter is friendly and mature.
- He uses words such as *character*, *experience*, *dependable* and *reliable* that give a sense of steadiness and stability without sounding too pompous for someone of his age.
- He emphasises his major strength – his existing professional driving skills. He emphasises that, although he is young, he has been driving for four years, has a lot of experience, and has a clean licence.

- His next major strength is his voluntary experience with the over-sixties' club. This suggests his ability to be patient and careful, and to get on with people very different from himself. Although this is not experience he has gained in paid employment, it is highly relevant to the vacancy for which he is applying.
- The fact that he does voluntary work also shows his willingness to work and his involvement in the community, important for someone in this sort of job.
- He describes himself as friendly and outgoing, requirements stated in the job advertisement and rephrased in Robert's own words.
- He gives a very good reason for applying for this job, and underlines his commitment and enthusiasm. The voluntary work that he does backs up his stated desire to work with people. So, too, does the fact that he has the initiative to read the *North & East Health Care Report* for vacancies.

53 Hillcroft Avenue
St Agnes Hill
Norwich
NR11 6LM

Tel: 00000 000000

14 February 2009

Ms Alice N Murray
Personnel Manager
St Agnes Patient Services Trust
St Agnes
Norwich
NR7 7SS

Dear Ms Murray

<u>Ref: PT/3 Driver, Patient Services Transport Driver</u>

I would like to apply for the position of Outpatient Transport Service Driver as advertised in this month's *North & East Health Care Report.*

I believe I have the character and the experience that you are looking for to fill this vacancy. I am an experienced driver with a full, clean licence, who also has good communication skills and relates well to people.

As you will see from the enclosed CV, I have been with Eastville Deliveries as a driver since acquiring my licence four years ago. During this time, I have also worked as a volunteer driver for the Wallwell over-sixties' club, a role that I have greatly enjoyed.

I am a friendly, outgoing person who is also dependable and reliable – I think Eastville would agree that my work record with them has been excellent. I am now, however, looking for a post with more contact with the public and feel that your advertisement offers just the opportunity that I am looking for.

I very much look forward to discussing my application with you in more detail, and I hope to hear from you in the near future.

Yours sincerely

Robert Catskill
Enc CV

Changing career

- When considering an applicant like Shirley, who is changing career, an employer might worry that:
  - she doesn't have the right skills and experience for the job;
  - she wouldn't understand what the job entails;
  - she wouldn't fit in with the organisation, having come from a different background;
  - the career change is a whim, and she will change again, or go back to her old job.

Shirley has answered many of these worries in her letter.

- She concentrates exclusively on the skills and experience that she has that match those required by the job. These are drawn from her voluntary work and the course that she is about to complete.
- She emphasises that she has both practical experience and theoretical knowledge, and this suggests that she will understand what the job requires.
- The content of her letter emphasises what she has learned and how she has developed. It suggests that these will be things that she will also encourage others to do. This could be an important part of the work she is hoping to do.
- She makes it very clear that she is starting a new career rather than looking for a different job. She has spent time and effort undergoing training and getting the necessary experience to qualify her for this.

30 May 2009

Mrs Janice Dean
Senior Co-ordinator
The Drake Trust
PO Box 7
Netherton
SX99 2QS

Dear Mrs Dean

I am writing in answer to your advertisement in today's *Woodshill Gazette* requesting applications for the position of Social Support Worker for young people with learning difficulties.

I believe that I have the skills and qualities that you are looking for. I am outgoing and open-minded, with many years' experience of relating to people with patience, respect and consideration. I am actively involved in the adult literacy and numeracy course at Woodshill Adult Education Centre and have experienced at first hand many of the problems that these young people face.

I am about to complete a one-year City & Guilds Counselling Skills course at the same Centre, and I am interested in the opportunity that this vacancy offers to complement my studies with real experience. I greatly enjoyed the course, which I feel has given me the chance to enlarge my interpersonal skills and competencies. It has, especially, given me an insight into the way that people can grow and develop.

I very much look forward, now, to taking these skills into the workplace in a professional capacity with an organisation offering the opportunity to work in my area of special interest.

I would welcome the occasion to discuss my application with you further and hope to hear from you in the near future.

I enclose my CV as requested.

Yours sincerely

Shirley J Pope
Enc CV

Lacking specific qualifications

- This is a job at a 24-hour recovery and repair garage. The advertisement asked for someone who was preferably a motor mechanic, or trained in motor vehicle repairs.
- Guy has no formal training, but is currently doing a very similar job at a smaller place for less pay and with less prospect of promotion.
- Guy rang the company to ask if it was still worth making an application even though he lacked one of the things they asked for. Hardy Vehicles said that they wanted someone with a knowledge of mechanics who would be able to talk intelligently to customers and maybe offer advice over the phone. They thought it would suit someone with mechanical skills who was trying to move into the customer service and management side of the business. Hardy's suggested that, if he wanted to apply, they would consider his application.

- Although not trained, Guy has picked up sufficient technical information from his current job to feel that he can answer the company's requirements. He has a good practical understanding of the business from the work that he is currently doing.
- He also feels that, as an experienced receptionist, he can actually offer them a better service than could someone new to this type of work.
- His letter concentrates on his skills with customers. He emphasises his knowledge and experience, and highlights his success to date. He has greatly improved customer loyalty at Lowe & Co – something in which most employers would be interested.
- Guy's letter picks up every point in his favour. It also emphasises his ambition and determination – he is interested in training and career development. This is in line with Hardy's statement that they are looking for someone who wants to develop further.
- Although he can't give them exactly what they want, Guy makes sure that he puts across what he *can* offer them with confidence and assurance. He may persuade them that the skills that he has would be of value to Hardy Vehicles, as long as he can adequately compensate for his lack of formal training.

144 Uddingley Hill
Four Miles
Kent
KN7 2AW

Tel: 00000 000000

10 March 2009

Mr Andrew King
Manager
Hardy Vehicles
Willings Road
Willington
Kent
KN1 1MM

Dear Mr King

Re: Central Service Receptionist

Please find enclosed my CV in application for the above position as advertised in yesterday's *Willington Journal.*

As you will see from my career details, I have extensive experience of customer service and reception work, and appreciate what a vital link customer reception is between the customer and the workshop.

I am a confident, friendly communicator with a mature and responsible outlook. I am currently employed by Lowe & Co, where my aim is to provide a quality service to clients. My greatest achievement to date has been to increase the number of customers returning for a second time by more than half.

During my time at Lowe & Co I have developed an appreciation for, and a good practical understanding of, the motor vehicle trade. In addition, I am well used to working shifts as I currently work a similar rota system and find it no problem.

I am keen to find a company offering full training and career development opportunities, and am, consequently, most interested in the vacancy that you have to offer.

I look forward to hearing from you.

Yours sincerely

Guy Sheppard
Enc CV

Lacking specific experience

- Weber Foods are looking for a delivery representative – someone who can deliver to existing clients, and also look for new clients and extra sales as they make their round. The job is mainly that of a delivery driver, but they have stated that some sales experience, though not essential, would be preferred.
- Ross is currently a delivery driver, but has no sales experience. He does, however, realise that he uses the skills that he would need as a sales representative in the voluntary work that he does – tact, persuasion, confidence, etc.
- Ross's letter focuses first on his skills and experience as a delivery driver. He emphasises the degree of responsibility that he has had, and his ability to organise himself and be self-motivated. These will be useful attributes in the job for which he is applying.
- He stresses his reliability and dependability, and describes himself as personable and confident. These are key words taken from the advertisement and rephrased by Ross.
- He goes on to highlight his work with the public and his skills in this area. He not only shows that he has the relevant experience, but also demonstrates that he understands and appreciates the skills needed.
- Ross closes with a statement of how happy he is in his present job, but that he is looking for a more challenging position. He sounds enthusiastic and motivated.

To see what happens as a result of Ross's letter, see Chapter 16, *Answering job offers*.

9 Old Meadow
East Inglestone
Gloucestershire
GL9 1VB

Tel: 00000 000000

3 July 2008

Mr Simon Jake
Personnel Manager
Weber Foods plc
Frow Trading Estate
Gloucester
GL11 7XC

Dear Mr Jake

Please find enclosed my CV in application for the position of Delivery Representative as advertised in today's *Gloucester Informer*.

I believe that I have many of the personal qualities that you ask for, along with an excellent driving record.

I have been a delivery driver with Hogg Supplies for the past five years, where I have organised my own round and been fully responsible for both planning and delivery on my route. During this time I have consistently and reliably performed my duties to the satisfaction of both Hogg and their customers alike.

I am self-reliant and dependable, as well as being personable and confident. I am well used to dealing with the public in my voluntary role as fund-raiser for the East Inglestone Children's Charity. As this entails approaching businesses and individuals for financial support, I have developed tact, persistence and the powers of persuasion over the years.

Although I have been very happy with Hogg, I am now looking for a position with more responsibility and greater scope for development. I believe that your vacancy offers just the opportunity that I am looking for in order to advance my career.

I would be very happy to discuss my application with you further and look forward to hearing from you.

Yours sincerely

Ross Walker
Enc CV

11

Applying for promotion

General points

Sometimes the job that you want to apply for is with your own company. You may be looking for internal promotion, or you may be reapplying for a position with the organisation after a takeover or merger.

It may feel strange to tell someone all about yourself when you think they know you already. But it's easy to take people for granted, so don't take any chances. Make sure they know what your skills, strengths and experience are, just as if you were applying to an unfamiliar employer.

The most important things that you can offer your employer when you are applying for an internal position are your knowledge of the company, and your familiarity with their way of doing things.

What you need to get across

Consider the following points for inclusion in your letter:

- your career history with the company and your progress with them;

- your current position, its duties and responsibilities;
- your knowledge of the company, its structure and organisation;
- your good relationship with current staff;
- your value to the company to date – point out your achievements;
- any skills and qualifications gained since your initial appointment by them;
- your reason for applying for the vacancy;
- your suitability for the post.

A letter to accompany an application form

- Julie opens with her current position and points out her excellent track record with the company to date.
- She gives her reasons for applying as being her readiness for more responsibility and challenge, qualities strongly emphasised in the job description.
- She tells them about the qualifications gained since her appointment, and emphasises their relevance to this new position.
- Julie then goes on to underline her other strengths, and her experience and understanding of the department.
- This is a large company with a personnel department, and requires a formal approach.
- Even though it is being sent to the personnel department, the letter is, nevertheless, addressed to a named individual.
- A completed application form is being sent with the letter, so 'Enc' needs to go at the end.

43 Goldcar Crescent
Hodbury
Kent
HD7 9JA

Tel: 00000 000000

6 August 2008

Jane Hallby
Personnel Manager
XTC Communications
West Gate
Hodbury
Kent
HD10 7JD

Dear Ms Hallby

Senior Data Administrator

Please find enclosed my application form for consideration for the above position. I have been Data Management Clerk for XTC Communications for the past two years and believe I have successfully demonstrated my ability, commitment and enthusiasm for the job during this time. I now feel ready and able to move on to a more responsible and challenging role.

Having recently passed City & Guilds 2370 Data Handling Level 3, I am well qualified to undertake the duties of the post. I feel sure that my organisational and interpersonal skills would also make a valuable contribution. The experience gained in my current position has given me an insight into the work of the department and, I believe, a thorough understanding of both the problems and possibilities of communication data handling.

Yours sincerely

Julie Franks
Enc

On the retirement of a colleague

- James opens with his reasons for making a speculative application.
- He goes on to mention his history with the company and emphasises his experience and suitability.
- He underlines his first-hand knowledge of the post and suggests a previous good relationship with the retiring employee.
- This letter reflects the fact that this is a small organisation where the people concerned know each other well.
- The letter just 'opens negotiations'; James may be asked to send in his CV or to present a formal application when the position officially comes up for consideration.
- There is a hint – 'I feel that now is a good time' – that James may move on elsewhere if promotion is not forthcoming.
- James has a current position with the company and includes this with his signature.

31 Lyonmead
Matley
North Yorks
NY14 3PU

Tel: 00000 000000

21 July 2008

Mr James Mander
Marketing Director
J-Bow Supplies Ltd
Unit 3
Marsh Cross
North Yorks
NY6 5SD

Dear Mr Mander

I was very sad to learn that Michael Knighton will be leaving us shortly due to his continuing ill health. We will all miss him greatly, both as a colleague and as a friend.

When you come to think about his replacement, may I ask you to consider me? I have, as you know, been with the company for 10 years now and have greatly enjoyed my work during that time, as well as gaining a wealth of experience. I feel that now is a good time for me to consolidate that experience by moving to a more senior position.

I think Michael would agree that my performance has been of a consistently high standard during our time together. I am confident, knowing what I do of his work, that I have the qualities of persistence and diligence necessary to fill this position.

Yours sincerely

James Gorstan
Assistant Marketing Manager

A speculative approach

- Sonia starts with her reasons for making this speculative approach. They show her enthusiasm and initiative.
- In her e-mail, she emphasises her current duties and responsibilities and has picked out the ones with the greatest similarity to those she will require as a Retail Supervisor.
- She has included her CV. This will give more background details about her work history and current responsibilities, so she doesn't need to go into them up front.
- She outlines her career progression with the company, subtly pointing out that they have promoted her before.
- She underlines her knowledge of the organisation.
- As this is a speculative letter, Sonia may need to make a formal application again when the new store opens.
- Even if plans for the new store fall through, Sonia will be on record with the personnel department as being interested in promotion.
- For more information about this type of letter, see Chapter 6, *Speculative letters*.

Staff for Hidgate
Sonya Pellow [spellow@anyisp.co.uk]
To: drush@laineretail.co.uk

Dear Mr Rush

I believe that Laine Retail are planning to open a new store in Hidgate in the new year. This being so, I would like you to consider me for the position of Retail Supervisor at the new site.

I am at present working at the Redgate shop as a Retail Assistant and have been in this post for the past two years. My current duties include:

- supervising temporary staff
- dealing with the public
- stock management
- display and merchandising.

I previously worked at the central warehouse as an order picker. During my time with Laine Retail I believe I have gained a thorough understanding of the organisation, together with the skills and experience necessary for the post of Retail Supervisor.

I look forward to hearing from you soon. My full CV follows.

Yours sincerely

Sonia Pellow
11 Dewsbury Court
Elsmead
Norfolk
NF2 5FP

spellow@anyisp.co.uk

Tel: 00000 000000

Requesting help or advice

General points

Friends and acquaintances can give you valuable help and advice when you are looking for a job. They can:

- give you background information on a particular field or profession;
- keep a look-out for any vacancies that might arise;
- give you names and addresses of others who might be able to help;
- put you in contact with people.

You may be hesitant about asking, but, on the whole, people like to help. Think how valued you would feel if someone came to you and asked for your advice.

You can write to:

- friends;
- acquaintances;

- relatives;
- people you were at school or college with;
- people you used to work with;
- members of organisations and associations;
- tutors/college lecturers;
- colleagues;
- business contacts;
- professionals in your field, or in allied fields;
- people you meet on business or training courses;
- people you meet at trade fairs;
- careers advisers;
- consultants.

Make it clear that you are asking for help and advice, not angling for a job. This takes the pressure off people and makes it easier for them to give you useful information. Don't worry; if they know of a suitable vacancy, they'll tell you about it anyway.

Whoever you are writing to, make sure that the letter doesn't look like a standard one that's being sent out to dozens of people. If possible, tailor the contents to the person concerned, but at least send the letter to a named individual. This is always important, but it's essential when you are asking someone for help.

As a general rule, letters to friends should be friendly, and letters to business people should be businesslike.

Keep your letter short, direct and to the point. Asking for help can be a bit embarrassing, and the temptation might be to try to disguise it with padding and waffle. However, this can be confusing and irritating for the recipient, who can't work out what they are being asked for, or how to respond.

Think about the sort of information, suggestions, names or contacts that you need before you write, so that you can give them some sort of idea of what would be useful to you. The clearer you are about what you need, the more likely you are to get a helpful reply.

Always follow up any contact names or referrals that you are given unless there is a very good reason not to do so. Always, too, follow up replies with letters of thanks, to let those who have helped you know what you did about their advice, and how it worked out. See Chapter 14, *Thank you letters*.

What you need to get across

Consider including the following points in your letter:

- The reason why you are writing – to ask for help and advice.
- The reason why you are writing at this time.
- The reason why you are writing to them in particular. Say why you are asking *them* for advice – maybe it's because of their knowledge, experience, good sense or good judgement.
- If it's a contact name or a referral from someone else, say who referred you, and why.
- Give a brief outline of your background, skills, qualifications and experience.
- Tell them how they can help you. Make it clear what advice or information you want; don't leave them to do all the work.
- Make your appreciation clear.
- If you intend to follow up the letter with a phone call, tell them so, and give some idea of when.

To a fellow member of an organisation

Henry is writing to the members of his professional association to ask them if they have any information on vacancies.

This is the type of letter that could be sent as e-mail if a substantial number of members are on the internet. The same request for information could be sent cheaply and quickly to a large number of people, and replying is equally quick and easy. He will prepare each one individually, though, and not just Cc a list of names.

- Note that he makes it clear that he is asking for recommendations, rather than asking for a job.
- Although a copy of the letter is being sent to every name on the organisation's mailing list, Henry still sends each one to a named individual.
- Those members that Henry knows well will receive a more personal letter, like the one on the next page.
- His opening sentence comes straight to the point, saying why he is writing, and the reason why he is writing to this particular person.
- He outlines who he is and his relevant career background, before going on to say why he needs help now.
- He states clearly that he wants contact names in his specific field.
- Henry closes by expressing his gratitude and appreciation.
- For the next stage, see Chapter 14, *Thank-you letters*.

43 East Parade
Oxhill
Devon
DV3 9EJ

Tel: 00000 000000

25 April 2009

Nell Sandiman
St Lawrence Associates
St Lawrence
Devon
DV6 8TH

Dear Ms Sandiman

I am writing to you as a fellow member of the Finance Circle to ask for your advice about possible job opportunities. As an executive with a broad background in financial administration, I am now looking for a permanent position within the field.

My 21 years' experience in finance includes five years in the design and implementation of accounting and management systems, and 16 years in accounts and data-processing. Sadly, the company that I currently work for is merging with another organisation and, as a result, my position will become redundant.

I wonder, therefore, if you could recommend any friends, associates or business contacts who may have a suitable opening for someone with my skills and experience?

I look forward to hearing from you, and I would greatly appreciate any information or advice that you can give me.

Yours sincerely

Henry Gilby

To a colleague in another company

This is Henry's letter to a colleague. As this is a friend, Henry addresses him by his first name rather than the more formal 'Mr Collins'.

- The tone is friendly, but it is still businesslike and straightforward.
- He goes into a little more detail about what has happened to cause him to be writing for help at this time.
- The information is a little more personal – he has had an offer from his present company, but he wants something better.
- As this is someone who has worked with him and knows him quite well, Henry doesn't need to state his skills and qualifications; Frank will be aware of them.
- He gives clear suggestions as to how Frank can help him.
- Henry intends to telephone him for a meeting, and tells him this so that Frank can prepare for it.

25 April 2009

Frank Collins
Ordale Holdings
Hinton Green
Hinton
BT7 7RR

Dear Frank

As you will have heard, the recent merger with Lang International has caused major upheavals here. Sadly, the department where I have worked for the past three years is to close at the end of the year. While the company has offered me the opportunity to work with them on a freelance basis, I would prefer something with more stability.

I am writing to ask for your help. While I don't expect you to come up with any immediate answers, I would greatly appreciate your keeping an ear to the ground for any likely openings in the near future. You know my general background and experience, and the sort of thing I would be looking for.

Perhaps you know of a company that needs someone like me? If you have any suggestions about anyone I could contact, I would be very grateful for your advice.

If you have time next week, I'd like to drop in to discuss any ideas you might have. I'll call you on Monday to see if it's convenient.

Yours sincerely

Henry Gilby

To a friend

This is an e-mail to a friend at her private address. Because of this, Marie uses her friend's first name only rather than addressing her as Ms Craig. Informal letters to friends can, of course, be sent by conventional mail, if this is more convenient.

- The tone is friendly and informal, but it still gets to the point.
- Marie tells Stephanie why she is writing, and why she is writing to her specifically – because of her knowledge and experience.
- As a friend, she shares some of her more personal feelings with her, her shock about what has happened, and her determination to come through it.
- She tells her exactly what help Stephanie can give her.
- She tells her that she will ring her, and closes with her gratitude and appreciation for what she hopes will be her friend's help.

- As this is a letter to a friend, Marie need only use her first name as a signature, rather than her full name. Compare this with Frank's signature to a business colleague in the last letter.

Help and advice
Marie Paul [mpaul@anyisp.co.uk]
To: scraig@myisp.uk

Dear Stephanie

I'm hoping that you may be able to give me some help and advice.

As you may know, the company that I work for was bought out last October, and as a result I am being made redundant. While it has been a great shock, I am determined to see this as an opportunity. I think a change has been due for some time, and this is my chance to explore new ideas.

One of the things I am considering is freelance work, and this is where I would very much appreciate your knowledge and experience.

If you are agreeable, I have some ideas that I would like the opportunity to explore with you and get your views on. I'd also be very grateful if you could suggest anyone else who you think it would be useful for me to contact. You meet such a wide range of people in your work, you may be aware of people who could use the skills I have to offer.

I'm very keen to talk to you and will call you in the next few days. I would greatly welcome your help, and look forward to talking things over with you.

Yours

Marie

Mentioning a mutual acquaintance

Julia is writing to Mrs Beck on the suggestion of Sarah Bourton. As this is a referral from someone else, Julia mentions Sarah's name by way of introduction.

- The tone of the letter is businesslike and direct, while also being courteous.
- She explains why she is writing, and why Mrs Beck's advice would be especially useful to her.
- She encloses her CV to give Mrs Beck her background information rather than including it in the letter. As she is thinking about a change of career, much of her experience will not be strictly relevant to residential care work and she doesn't really need to emphasise it.
- Julia explains precisely what information most interests her, but also suggests that she is open to general advice.
- She tells Mrs Beck clearly that she would like to meet her to discuss things, and says that she will phone for an appointment.
- 'Enc CV' tells Mrs Beck that Julia has included her CV with the letter.

For what happens next, see Chapter 14, *Thank-you letters*.

23 June 2008

Mrs Glenda Beck
Principal Care Officer
Rydebank House
Saunton
Shropshire
SY19 7PP

Dear Mrs Beck

Sarah Bourton suggested that I write to you for information about working in Residential Care. As I am presently hoping to develop my career, I am looking for all the help and advice available. I understand from Sarah that this is your special area and so your advice would be especially helpful.

I have enclosed my CV to give you an idea of my skills and experience to date, and I would very much welcome the opportunity to discuss these with you further.

I would be grateful for any information you may be able to give me. Your knowledge of the field and experience with this type of work make any suggestions you may have extremely valuable. I would also welcome any ideas you may have about the future opportunities and prospects for employment in the field.

I would appreciate the chance to meet you. I'll telephone early next week to see if an appointment can be arranged.

Yours sincerely

Julia Harris

Enc CV

To a former course tutor

- Elizabeth first introduces herself in her letter – it is probable that a course tutor will have seen many students. Giving the year is helpful; her tutor may want to look up her past file before recommending her to anybody.

- She thanks her tutor for what she has already done and lets her know how it has turned out.
- Having told her what she hopes to do, Elizabeth goes on to ask for Margaret Hedges' assistance.
- She explains why she has chosen her – her network of contacts – and suggests a way in which she could help.
- As well as enclosing her CV for background information, Elizabeth sets out her most important skills in the letter. She does this in such a way that they can be seen at a glance.
- The tone of the letter manages to be both courteous and efficient, reflecting the qualities of a good administrator.
- Elizabeth closes with her intention to follow this letter up with a phone call.
- She remembers to put 'Enc CV' after her signature to indicate that her CV is enclosed.

See Chapter 14, *Thank you letters,* for what happens next.

43 Church Crescent
Pointcross
Kent
KN4 4RD

Tel: 00000 000000

20 January 2009

Mrs Margaret Hedges
School of Business Studies
Cairn College
East Lowell
West Sussex
SU8 8NB

Dear Mrs Hedges

You may remember me from the 2005–2006 Business Administration course. I enjoyed the course enormously at the time, and the diploma I gained guaranteed a successful start to my career. Since then I have worked extensively in administration for both private and public companies. I feel that now is a good time for me to consolidate that experience by moving to a position offering more responsibility and challenge.

This is where I am hoping that you can help me. I am sure that you must have built up an extensive network of contacts during your time in the department. I wonder if you would be able to suggest anyone who would be interested in the skills and experience that I have to offer? I have enclosed my CV to give you an idea of the type of work I have done since leaving college. Briefly, my skills include:

- compiling reports;
- attending meetings and taking minutes;
- arranging appointments;
- attending to customer enquiries;
- dealing with correspondence;
- ordering stationery and consumables.

I would be very grateful for any advice or information you might be able to give me.

If you have the time, I would very much like to come in and discuss the possibilities with you. I will call in the next week or so to see if a convenient time can be arranged.

Yours sincerely

Elizabeth Lawrence
Enc CV

Asking a friend to put in a good word

Tina is e-mailing a friend and former colleague who works at the company that she has just applied to. An e-mail like this could, of course, be just as easily sent as an informal letter.

- She explains her situation briefly, and suggests how Mark could help her. Note that she doesn't express this as a request, but in terms of the value that she would put on Mark's help.
- She reminds him of their friendship, and their former good working relationship. If she gets the appointment, they may be working together again.
- She gives Mark a clear idea of how he can help her, but leaves the details open so as not to seem demanding or pressing.
- She emphasises value and gratitude throughout.
- Tina closes on a friendly and personal note.

> Support valued
> Tina Morris [tmorris@anyisp.co.uk]
> To: mparker@anyisp.uk
>
> Dear Mark
>
> I am applying for the position of Customer Services Manager with Inge & Haroldsby and I would greatly value any support that you could give my application.
>
> We have known each other for a good many years now, and have worked well together in the past. I hope that you feel that you would be able to put in a good word for me if the occasion arose. There's no need to tell you how extremely grateful I would be.
>
> Good luck in the tournament, by the way. Give me a call and let me know how you got on.
>
> Yours
>
> Tina

Asking for an introduction

Terry is e-mailing a business colleague, Paul, to ask for a letter of introduction. In a previous conversation, Paul has mentioned to Terry that a colleague of his has a vacancy coming up, and might be interested in someone with Terry's background.

- Terry explains the situation briefly, reminds Paul about their conversation, and suggests how Paul can help.
- He states very clearly what he wants: a letter of introduction.
- His e-mail emphasises his enthusiasm for Paul's idea.
- He closes on a note of thanks.

Introduction to Nigel Jukes
Terry Heath [theath@anyisp.co.uk]
To: pmonott@anyisp.uks

Dear Paul

I have been thinking about our conversation last week, and I wonder if you would be kind enough to give me a letter of introduction to Nigel Jukes at Portland Holdings. I will be in that area in July and the opportunity seems too good to miss.

You mentioned at the time that he might be interested in someone from a petrochemical background, and I should very much like to see him.

Thank you, in anticipation.

Yours

Terry

13

Follow-up letters

General points

Applying for jobs takes time and effort, so make the most of the work you have already done. Build on the impression you have made and improve your impact – follow up all your contacts with a letter.

Send follow-up letters after:

- phone calls;
- interviews;
- informal meetings;
- rejections;
- a long silence.

The purpose of the letter is to:

- say thank you;
- give more information about yourself;
- update information;
- expand on topics that came up;

- confirm anything that was said;
- get things on record;
- underline your interest.

When you are looking for a job, there is often a lot to be gained from building up a good relationship with a few organisations. Often, this is a better strategy than spreading your campaign thinly around as many companies as you can reach. Find the organisations who do the sort of work that you want, and target your serious efforts at them.

There is evidence to suggest that 80 per cent of your results will come from only 20 per cent of your contacts. So decide which letters, phone calls and meetings have had the most positive or promising response. Concentrate your activity there, and only move on to the other 80 per cent when you have thoroughly covered the most responsive 20 per cent.

What you need to get across

Consider including the following points in your letter:

- Write to the person who you have seen or spoken to, not to the personnel department.
- Say what contact you have had – a letter, a telephone call, an interview, whatever.
- Include any relevant details such as any job title, or the department involved.
- Thank them for their time and attention.
- Recap the relevant points of your last conversation.
- Confirm any points that may have been decided.
- Introduce any new and relevant information that you want to give them.

Confirming an interview

Donald's letter of application to Dutch Industrial for the position of Stock Records Clerk is included in Chapter 8, *Starting again*.

- The company have written to Donald offering him an interview for the job, and he is writing back confirming that he will be attending.
- Always write or phone to confirm interviews when possible, rather than just turning up on the day. Otherwise, the company may be uncertain whether you have received their letter, or they may just take your lack of response for a lack of interest.
- The letter is straightforward, and includes the job title, reference number, and the time and date of the interview.
- If Donald had been unable to attend at the time suggested, he would have rung them to arrange another time and then written a similar letter to confirm the new time.
- If he was no longer interested in the job, or had already taken another one, he would have written back to Dutch Industrial to tell them this. There is a letter declining a job offer that you could adapt for this purpose in Chapter 16, *Answering job offers*.
- Even in this short, businesslike letter, Donald manages to sound friendly, polite and enthusiastic.

Flat 3
Hunt House
Deansgate
Wellings
Hertfordshire
HE10 6ZA

Tel: 00000 000000

2 April 2009

Mr E J Fenn
Personnel Manager
Dutch Industrial
Unit 7
Impney Industrial Estate
Impney
Hertfordshire
HE19 9BV

Dear Mr Fenn

Re: Stock Records Clerk, Reference Vac/SR3/Het

Thank you for your letter of the 30 March 2009. I shall be pleased to attend an interview at the above address on Monday 12 April at 11.00 am. I look forward to meeting you then.

Yours sincerely

Donald Rice

Following a telephone call

Sam wrote to Julian Vell following a conversation with him at a business exhibition. You can find her original letter in Chapter 6, *Speculative letters*.

- As suggested in that section, she followed up her letter with a phone call to him. The call went very well. Julian Vell was very informative about the new intranet system, and interested in Sam's experience of introducing a similar system for another company.

- Sam now follows up with another letter to him, thanking him for his time and recapping the main features of the call.
- The main purpose of her letter is to underline the similarity between the situation that Astra will be facing and the difficulties that she has successfully handled at County Trust.
- Astra are only at the planning stage of the operation at the moment; they will not be needing someone like Sam until the scheme is much more advanced.
- Sam will contact them again in a couple of months to see what progress they have made, and to find out if they are now ready to think about employing someone with her skills.
- Sam has made good use of that chance meeting at the business exhibition. She has also written to several other people who were there, and she has high hopes for the future.

28 September 2008

Mr Julian Vell
Astra Finance
Astra House
Wellings Road
Derby
DB9 7HW

Dear Mr Vell

Thank you for taking the time to talk to me on the phone yesterday about your company's plans with regard to information technology. It really does seem to be a major undertaking, but very exciting nonetheless.

You seem to be facing the same sort of situation that County Trust found themselves in some time ago. I know that, in their case, the introduction of networked systems solved many of their problems.

> I would very much like to talk to you further when your plans are a little more advanced. I believe that I have skills and experience that would be extremely useful to you during the change-over, and which could smooth the process considerably.
>
> I will call you again in due course to keep in touch with the situation.
>
> Yours sincerely
>
> Sam Tarrent

Following a meeting

Angus sent a speculative e-mail to Kore Pharmaceuticals, outlining his familiarity with the sort of work that they are doing, and suggesting a short meeting. The letter is in Chapter 6, *Speculative letters*. He is now writing to them, following that meeting, to thank them and to comment positively on the company and its methods.

- The main thing that he wants to get across is his interest in the processes they are using, as well as his valuable experience.
- During their meeting, Anne Carter has told him that she is not recruiting at the moment. However, there is a strong probability that the company will continue to expand, and that she will need people in the future.
- Although Angus doesn't refer to this directly, he confirms that he is interested in any jobs that may come up. Given his experience, he would be thinking about a reasonably senior position, but he doesn't go into details at this stage.
- He will call again in a couple of months to see what the situation is.

Meeting 17 Sep 2008
Angus Hanshaw [ahanshaw@anyisp.co.uk]
To: acarter@korepharm.com

Dear Mrs Carter

Thank you for taking the time to see me yesterday, I found our talk most enjoyable and informative.

I was particularly interested to note the innovative production techniques that you are currently using. These certainly promise to improve the quality of the final product.

May I say that, should you decide to take on extra staff for this project, I would be very interested in being considered.

I believe the experience that I have to date could be valuable to you, and that I could be a useful team member. I will call you again, if I may, to keep in touch with the situation.

Yours sincerely

Angus Hanshaw
43 Bowes Lane
Edinburgh
EH5 4PQ
ahanshaw@anyisp.co.uk
Tel: 0000 000 0000

Updating a speculative letter

When you have sent out speculative letters to people, it is a good idea to update them at regular intervals. This not only lets them know that you are still interested in finding another position, it also gives you the opportunity to tell them about any new skills or experience that you may have acquired in the meantime.

- The first letter that Vita sent to Rex Gambler met with little response. When she rang them to follow it up, they told her that they were not taking on any more staff under any circumstances at that time.

- Things have improved since then, and Vita is approaching them again to see if they are starting to recruit.
- She has filled her time, meanwhile, by adding to her capabilities with a further course of training at an evening class. These are skills relevant to the sort of job she is looking for.
- This means that she is able to write them a positive letter telling them how she is even more suitable for the job, rather than having to say that she is still searching for a better position.
- As well as telling them what she has been doing, Vita has sent them a new, updated CV for them to keep on file. Most companies will keep CVs on file for about six months to a year. If they haven't heard from you again during this time, they will probably scrap your CV the next time that file is sorted out and updated. Even CVs on computer data files are subject to editing, and there's no guarantee your key words will still be relevant next time a scan is run.

12 Henshaw Crescent
Upper Tithing
Northamptonshire
NP18 6AL

Tel: 00000 000000

30 April 2009

Mrs Julia Crabb
Department Head
Rex Gambler
Ascot House
Cartwright Place
Hills Barton
Northamptonshire
NP7 7HB

Dear Mrs Crabb

Since last writing to you I have further upgraded my skills with a course on computer accounting using the Addition

Accountant system. This included modules on sales, purchases and nominal ledgers, producing reports, audit trails and VAT procedures, among others.

I have enclosed an updated CV giving full details of this as well as my background and experience to date.

I would very much welcome the opportunity to talk to you again to see what opportunities may have arisen during the past six months.

I will call your office during the next week to see when would be convenient for a short discussion about the current situation.

Yours sincerely

Vita Sharp
Enc CV

After an interview: Expressing thanks and interest

- While it's not essential, it is always a good idea to follow up an interview with a letter. This can be just to express your thanks for their time, or you could use it as an opportunity to include, or highlight, further information.
- Send the letter promptly after the interview, and send it to the person who did the interviewing. If you were interviewed by more than one person, you could either send a letter to each person, send it to the most senior person, or – probably the best – send it to the person you already have contact with.
- If the person with whom you have established contact is not the person who interviewed you – in the case of a speculative approach, for example – send them a short letter at the same time. Thank them for their help, and let them know how you got on.

- Robert has just been interviewed for the job as Outpatient Transport Services Driver, and is writing to thank Alice Murray. She is the personnel officer who interviewed him, and to whom he sent his original letter of application. This letter can be found in Chapter 10, *Troubleshooting*.
- He explains what he got out of the interview, and emphasises that as he now has a better knowledge of the job, he is even more sure that it is the right one for him.

53 Hillcroft Avenue
St Agnes Hill
Norwich
NR11 6LM

Tel: 00000 000000

2 March 2009

Ms Alice N Murray
Personnel Manager
St Agnes Patient Services Trust
St Agnes
Norwich
NR7 7SS

Dear Ms Murray

Thank you for interviewing me for the post of Outpatient Transport Service Driver yesterday, Monday 1 March 2009. I greatly appreciated the opportunity to meet you.

During the interview I felt I gained a deeper understanding of the responsibilities of the job. It was very interesting to see in more detail how the Outpatient Transport Service fits into the wider picture of patient care.

I believe that this is exactly the sort of position that I am looking for, and I hope that you will consider that I have the character and experience necessary to make a useful contribution.

I look forward to hearing from you.

Yours sincerely

Robert Catskill

After an interview: Including more information

- Lilian is e-mailing Dr Miller after her interview.
- Her letter strongly emphasises her interest in the job, and her confidence in her ability to do it.
- She also includes further information about her skills and experience that are relevant to this position. She has noticed that the clinic uses a database system that she is familiar with, having used it before. This knowledge would help her to adapt to the new job quickly and efficiently, and is another point in her favour.
- It also confirms her interest during her visit to the clinic. Lilian took notice of what she was seeing, and thought about what it meant.
- The whole tone of her letter is confident and efficient as well as friendly, demonstrating the qualities she will need in the job.

Interview
Lilian Daniels [ldaniels@anyisp.co.uk]
To: cmiller@pittwalker.co.uk

Dear Dr Miller

Thank you for interviewing me for the position of Clinic Manager, yesterday, Friday 13 February 2009.

Having heard about the work in more detail, I feel that I could make a significant contribution to the Clinic. My current experience as an Assistant Departmental Manager has developed my management skills to the high level required by your organisation.

I should also add that I noticed when being shown around yesterday that you use a V-Max database system. I have extensive knowledge of this system having used the 2.1 version at Erskine-Lewis for two and a half years.

I would welcome the opportunity of working with your team and look forward to hearing from you.

Yours sincerely

Lilian Daniels
9 Dunkley Road
Broadwall
Essex
BR13 8XJ
ldaniels@anyisp.co.uk
Tel: 00000 000000

After an interview: Including references

- Jane has just been interviewed for her first job. You can see her letter of application to Benn, Hodge & Keen in Chapter 7, *Getting started.*
- They have, rather unusually, asked her to obtain her own references and send them in to the office.
- Jane is sending two references. One is from her course tutor, talking about her work and qualifications. The other is a personal reference about her character from the leader of the youth club that she has attended for the past three years, and where she often helps out.
- The covering letter that she sends with the references uses the opportunity to confirm her interest in the job and in what she has seen of the company.
- She points out the good match between her interests and the company's interests, and highlights her commitment and enthusiasm.
- The tone of her letter is positive and assured, as well as friendly and polite.

10 May 2008

Mr Tony Crispin
Department Head
Benn, Hodge & Keen
Market Square
Dean
Surrey
SR2 7JJ

Dear Mr Crispin

Thank you for interviewing me for the position of Administration Assistant on Wednesday. I enjoyed the interview and was glad to be given the chance to see the working of a financial agency at first hand.

May I say that I would be very interested in taking this position with your company. It offers the opportunity that I am looking for to develop a career in administration that also combines my special interest in finance. I believe that, in time, I could make a significant contribution to Benn, Hodge & Keen, and I hope that you will consider my application favourably.

I enclose my references as you request, and look forward to hearing from you soon.

Yours sincerely

Jane Clark
Encs

After rejection: Following an interview

Although it is a very hard thing to do, it is often worthwhile sending a follow-up letter to companies that have rejected you. By doing so, you maintain the good impression that you have worked hard to build up. There may be other opportunities in the future, or you may want their help and advice again at a later date.

- Angela has been turned down for the position of Personal Assistant that she was interviewed for. Her application letter for this post can be seen Chapter 5, *Answering advertised vacancies.*
- She is now writing in reply, expressing her disappointment and, perhaps more importantly, her continuing interest in the company.
- By asking them to keep her on file, she may get to know of another job before they advertise it generally. Apex must have thought well of her to interview her in the first place, and another time she may be more successful.
- Angela could also consider ringing Paula Wing to ask where she fell short in either her skills and experience, or her performance at the interview. This would give her useful information about improving her presentation in the future. It may mean that she needs to improve her qualifications, or simply brush up her interview techniques.

Ground Floor Flat
47 Randall Road
South Tipping
Berkshire
BK11 8RM

Tel: 00000 000000

18 February 2008

Mrs Paula Wing
Personnel Manager
Apex Group
Apex House
Ringway
Berkshire
BK2 2OL

Dear Mrs Wing

<u>Ref: JJ/9/SSB Personal Assistant</u>

Thank you for your letter of 6 March 2008. Although I am disappointed at not being chosen for the post of Personal Assistant, I would like to thank you for taking the time to consider my application.

What I saw of the company at the interview interested me greatly, and I would still like the opportunity to work for you. I would, therefore, like to ask if you would keep my name and details on file for consideration should another vacancy arise.

Yours sincerely

Angela Price

After rejection: Following a speculative letter and phone call

- Michael has sent a speculative letter to Bower-Peal Financial Services, and followed this up with a phone call to discuss possible openings. They have now written back to say that they have no suitable vacancies at the present time. Michael's original letter to them can be seen in Chapter 6, *Speculative letters*.

- Michael is following up, again, to let them know that he is still interested in the organisation, and would like them to keep his name on file for the future. Their situation may change over the next few months, and Michael's details will be on hand should a vacancy arise.
- His letter demonstrates his understanding of the situation, but is still quietly assertive. He feels confident that he could be of use to Bower-Peal, and he emphasises this in his letter.

18 Clementine Square
High Grange
Surrey
SR23 9CS

Tel: 00000 000000

12 September 2008

Ms Maria Derby
Sales Director
Bower-Peal Financial Services
Columbus Way
London W4 7HH

Dear Ms Derby

Thank you for your letter of 10 September.

Having spoken to you on the telephone and heard about the company in more detail, I feel that I could make a significant contribution to Bower-Peal. I believe that my current experience as a Sales Manager has developed my management skills to the high level required by your organisation.

I recognise that the current economic climate has severely limited the opportunities that you have available. Would it be possible, however, for you to keep my name and details on file for consideration should a suitable vacancy occur within your company in the future?

Yours sincerely

Michael Franks

Reminder: Following an interview

It is often well worth sending out reminders to people and organisations that you haven't heard from for some time.

Keep in regular contact with people to whom you have sent speculative letters, and update them from time to time. Even if they have not contacted you, write to remind them of your continued interest.

If you are expecting to hear from somebody, after an interview, for example, and they don't get in contact, it is important for your own peace of mind to find out what is happening. Few people will mind a gentle prompting. While patience may be a virtue, too much can begin to look like indifference. Some companies, however, state that if you haven't heard from them within, say, a month, you are to assume you have not got the position.

- Linda has applied for a job as Deputy Catering Manager. You can find her application letter in Chapter 5, *Answering advertised vacancies*.
- She was interviewed for the position in May, and is concerned that a month has elapsed without any response. She is, consequently, writing to them to find out what is happening.
- Linda opens her letter with a reminder of her application, and a restatement of her interest in the job.

- She then goes on to remind them that she has heard nothing further from them, expressing her disappointment and puzzlement at this.
- She continues with a further reminder of her interest in them. She asks them to keep her name on file even if they have chosen someone else for the job.
- Her letter is polite and considerate, and it should achieve its purpose of prompting Anchorage Inns to tell her what is happening. If they haven't yet chosen anyone for the post, her interest may be a valuable point in her favour.

28 June 2008

Mr Peter Cox
Personnel Manager
Anchorage Inns Ltd
Kelmsley Place
Lambton
Oxfordshire
OX14 2HQ

Dear Mr Cox

Thank you for interviewing me for the post of Deputy Catering Manager on Wednesday 26 May. I greatly appreciated the opportunity to meet you and to see how a leading nationwide catering enterprise operates.

During the interview I felt I gained a deeper understanding of the scope of the job. It was very interesting to see in more detail how family entertainment and themed restaurants are developing in this country.

I believe that this is exactly the sort of position that I am looking for, and I am, naturally, disappointed to have heard nothing further from you.

I am hoping that this just means that you haven't reached a final decision yet, but I appreciate that it may mean that you have selected someone else for the job.

Though I would be disappointed at not being chosen for the post, I was very interested in what I saw of the company at the interview, and would still like the opportunity to work for you.

I would, therefore, request that you keep my name and details on file should another suitable vacancy arise.

Yours sincerely

Linda Vernon

Reminder: Following a speculative letter and a phone call

- Allison is writing to remind Kevin Walker that she is still interested in working for Willings & South, even though they haven't been in contact with her since March.
- Allison's original letter to them can be found in Chapter 6, *Speculative letters*, and her reply to an unsuitable offer from another company can be seen in Chapter 16, *Answering job offers*.
- She uses the letter as an opportunity to remind them briefly of her skills, qualities, and experience. These haven't changed significantly in the past three months, so there is little point in sending them a new CV – the company will still have her original one.
- She closes by saying that she will phone them shortly. The last conversation that they had was informative even if it was not especially productive. The company's situation could have changed in the meantime, and Allison might be more successful.

Ash Cottage
Tovey Lane
Tillington
Berkshire
BR17 4DF

Tel: 00000 000000

7 June 2008

Mr Kevin Walker
Personnel Director
Willings & South
Terrence Place
London
EC1 1FF

Dear Mr Walker

I wrote to you in March regarding the possibility of openings for office personnel with your company. The conversation that we had at that time was most interesting and informative, and gave a good insight into the organisation. I am now writing to you again to see if any opportunities have arisen in the meantime.

I am a fully qualified office supervisor with a sound background in administration and many years' experience of general office practice. I believe that I have the skills and competencies that fit well with your needs for first-rate office staff, and that I could make a valuable contribution to Willings & South.

I will call your office during the next week to see when would be convenient for a short discussion about the current situation.

Yours sincerely

Allison Tripp

14

Thank-you letters

General points

It's always a good idea to write to the people who have helped you to thank them for their assistance.

As well as expressing your gratitude, take the opportunity to tell them what is happening in your search. Let them know what you have done with the information or advice that they have given you, and how things worked out.

People like to be helpful, and they will enjoy sharing in your success. Write with a positive attitude, and tell friends and colleagues who have offered you their time, information or advice what you have built on that foundation.

What you need to get across

Think about including some of the following points in your thank you letters:

- your thanks and gratitude;
- how, exactly, they have been helpful to you;
- the result of their help;

- how your job search is going so far;
- what you intend to do next.

To a friend for help and advice

The following example is Julia's letter of thanks to Sarah for her advice. See Chapter 12, *Requesting help or advice*, for the start of the story, where Julia writes to Mrs Beck at Rydebank House on Sarah's suggestion.

- As this is a letter to a friend, the tone is friendly and informal.
- Julia tells Sarah exactly what she has done to follow up her suggestions.
- She tells her that they have met with a positive and helpful response, and outlines what has happened as a result.
- Julia closes with an expression of her gratitude.

3 Severn Road
Shorthill
Avon
AN7 7FF

Tel: 00000 000000

23 June 2008

Sarah Bourton
68 Bishop's Way
Sudley
Birmingham
BH12 4ZS

Dear Sarah

I'm just writing to say thank you for your help during my search for a new job. I've followed up a number of your suggestions, and have met with a very positive and helpful response.

Dr Hillforth has written back with some ideas about professional associations that might be of help; and James Donaldson has agreed to see me for an informal chat next week.

I've also been to see Mrs Beck at Rydebank House. She was very kind and encouraging, and most informative about prospects in this region. She has promised to keep my CV on file, and to let me know if she hears of anything.

Thank you again for your support.

Yours

Julia

For an informative meeting

At the same time as writing to Sarah to thank her for her suggestions, Julia has also written to Mrs Beck to thank her for her help. For the start of this story, see Chapter 12, *Requesting help or advice,* where Julia first writes to Mrs Beck for her advice.

Now she is writing to thank her for taking the time to see her informally, and for giving her a better, and more realistic, idea of the sort of job that she hopes to do.

- Julia outlines what it was that she has found helpful.
- The information that Mrs Beck has given her will help Julia to write speculative letters to potential employers, and to make more informed applications for the jobs that she sees advertised.
- She goes on to say how she has followed up Mrs Beck's suggestions.
- Julia closes with an expression of her gratitude.

3 Severn Road
Shorthill
Avon
AN7 7FF

Tel: 00000 000000

23 June 2008

Mrs Glenda Beck
Principal Care Officer
Rydebank House
Saunton
Shropshire
SY19 7PP

Dear Mrs Beck

Thank you for seeing me on Tuesday. I very much appreciate your taking time from your busy schedule to discuss working in residential care with me. Your advice and ideas have been a great help, and you have given me a much more realistic picture of the prospects on which I can base my job search.

I have written to the Bruce McKenna Trust as you suggested and am awaiting a reply.

Thank you again for your support. I very much appreciate your help and advice.

Yours sincerely

Julia Harris

For contact names

Henry is e-mailing a fellow member of his professional association to thank her for her help and information. Henry's first letter, asking for her help, is included in Chapter 12, *Requesting help or advice*.

- He thanks Nell Sandiman for sending him a list of names and addresses that he can either contact for more information, or to whom he can send speculative letters.

- His tone is enthusiastic and positive throughout, and he tells her what he has already done to follow up her suggestions.
- He closes with an offer to return the favour. Nell is a colleague and, in Henry's view, colleagues are people who help each other.

> Contact thanks
> Henry Gilby [hgilby@anyisp.co.uk]
> To: nsandiman@stlawrence.co.uk
>
> Dear Ms Sandiman
>
> Thank you for taking the time to send me your list of contact names and addresses. I very much appreciate your help and will lose no time in following up your suggestions. I have already contacted Daniel Hunt and Karen Malling, and I hope to be meeting them in the near future.
>
> i am extremely grateful for your help, and if there is ever anything I can do for you to return the favour, please let me know.
>
> Yours sincerely
>
> Henry Gilby

For information and advice

Elizabeth is writing to her former tutor, Margaret Hedges, to thank her for the help she has given her. You can see Elizabeth's letter asking for advice from Margaret in Chapter 12, *Requesting help or advice.*

Elizabeth had a short meeting with her to talk over the job market in general. Following this, Margaret sent her some names and addresses of contacts. Elizabeth wrote speculative letters to them, using Margaret's name as an introduction.

- In this letter, Elizabeth tells her how she has followed up her advice and help, and what has happened since.

- The result has been very rewarding. Elizabeth tells her about the job offer and expresses her delight.
- She also gives more details about the ways in which she believes Margaret's advice has helped her to get the job.
- The tone of the letter is one of pleasure, enthusiasm and gratitude.

43 Church Crescent
Pointcross
Kent
KN4 4RD

Tel: 00000 000000

7 March 2009

Mrs Margaret Hedges
School of Business Studies
Cairn College
East Lowell
West Sussex
SU8 8NB

Dear Mrs Hedges

I am writing to thank you for the information that you sent me shortly after our meeting back in January.

I sent my CV to Gilbert Anderson at Sherringham & Stapeley, as you suggested. He wrote back offering me an interview the following week, and I'm delighted to say that they have offered me a job as Personal Assistant.

Can I say, once again, how much I appreciate your help and encouragement during my recent job search. Your advice proved to be extremely valuable. It was not only the contact names that were important, but the background information as well. This gave me some interesting insights on which to base my approaches to organisations. I don't think I could have presented myself nearly so confidently to Sherringham & Stapeley if it hadn't been for that.

Thank you, again, for your support.

Yours sincerely

Elizabeth Lawrence

15

Asking for a reference

General points

When your job application has been successful, most employers will ask for your references. They will usually do this after the final interview, but before officially offering you the job.

You will have already given them the names and addresses of two people willing to give you a reference – your referees – either on your CV or on your application form.

It's usual to give two referees. One, usually your current or your most recent employer, who can vouch for your work record; and one, often a friend, who knows you well enough to comment on your character.

Your prospective employer will write to whoever you name as your referee, but it is a good idea for you to write to them first. Ask permission to use their name, and alert them to the fact that they may be asked to supply a reference for you.

What you need to get across

Consider the following points for inclusion in your letter:

- your request for a reference;
- your reason for asking this particular person to write it;

- a reminder of who you are – particularly for people you haven't worked with for some time, or if you work for a very large organisation;
- a brief description of the job you have applied for, so that they can write your reference to suit it;
- your enthusiasm for the new position;
- reassurance – particularly if you are asking for a reference from your current employer;
- a reminder of your qualities, strengths and achievements;
- a reminder of the good relationship you have enjoyed with your referee and the rest of the staff – if true;
- your gratitude for this service.

From a current employer

- Robert is writing to his current employer requesting a reference in connection with a job that he has recently applied for.
- Unusually, his prospective employers are asking for references from all their shortlisted candidates before the final interview. They need the letter quite soon, so that the interviews are not held up.
- He has already mentioned to George Hodges, unofficially, that he has applied for a more senior position with another company. This is usually a good idea; you don't want the request for a reference to come as a complete surprise.
- Robert specifically asks for a letter of recommendation, rather than a reference. The difference is subtle, but it sounds much more positive.
- He reassures his current employer that he is not unhappy, nor is he being disloyal, he just wants to better his prospects. Most employers accept with good grace that staff

will move on if they get a better offer, but Robert makes sure that there will be no ill-feeling if his application is unsuccessful, and he has to stay on at Northover.

- Robert reminds George that his work has always been good and that, consequently, he expects a good reference from him.

41 Wheat's Way
Ippingham
Buckinghamshire
BH19 2UU

Tel: 00000 000000

5 June 2008

Mr George Hodges
Department Manager
Northover Engineering
Verne Estate
Torden
Buckinghamshire
BH3 7TG

Dear Mr Hodges

I have applied for a position with Wallstone Aggregates and have passed the first interview. Wallstone require me to send them references before the final interview, and I would be very grateful if you could supply a letter of recommendation for this purpose.

While I am not unhappy in my current job, this new post is a senior position and offers greater opportunity for development. I can guarantee, however, that whether my application is successful or not, it will in no way compromise my loyalty to Northover.

I believe that my work here has always been of the highest standard and hope that you would feel able to reflect this in any reference that you may write.

Yours sincerely

Robert Wendover

From a former employer

- Charles is asking for a reference from a former employer.
- He mentions the job he has applied for, and then goes on to give his reason for particularly wanting a reference from Heartfield.
- So that Heartfield's will know, broadly, what the reference should cover, Charles tells them it is similar to the job that he did with them. He also mentions, however, that it is a more senior position.
- He reminds them that his work with them was of a high standard, and that he would expect them to give him a good reference. Heartfield should contact Charles and let him know if they feel unable to give him the sort of reference that he believes he deserves.
- He closes the letter with an expression of his gratitude.

Flat 3
15 Torworth Crescent
Everdean
Derbyshire
DB8 2GN

Tel: 00000 000000

6 June 2009

Mrs Shirley Wills
Personnel Manager
Heartfield Enterprises Ltd
Wood Heath
Norfolk
NF17 7FM

Dear Mrs Wills

I have recently been interviewed for the position of accounts manager for Eastbrook & Lisle of Henshaw. As I worked at Heartfield for some years, I would very much like to be able to put your name forward as a reference for myself and the quality of my work.

The duties of this new post are broadly similar to those I undertook during my time with you, but at a more senior level. They offer excellent prospects and the opportunity for future development.

I believe that my work at Heartfield was always of a consistently high standard, and I hope that you would feel able to reflect this in any reference that you may write.

I would, of course, be very grateful for your help in this matter.

Yours sincerely

Charles Morris

For a school leaver

- Anne is asking for a reference for her first full-time job.
- It can sometimes be difficult to find an employer who is able to give you a work reference if you have never worked full time before. Anne has done a Saturday job for a reasonably long time, and is able to give Brian Southwood as a referee.
- If you need a reference for your first job and haven't worked before, you could ask your school or college to give you a reference instead. Check with them who they would expect the request for a reference to be sent to – your tutor, your head of department or the head of school.
- Although the job that Anne has applied for is not very similar to the work that she has been doing at Southwood's Stores, Brian Southwood will be able to give a general reference for her, and confirm that she has had work experience.
- Anne will also ask a friend of the family who has known her for many years to give her a character reference and say what she is like as a person.

11 St Aldwyn's Road
Hill Crest
Hertfordshire
HR21 9BO

Tel: 00000 000000

18 August 2008

Mr Brian Southwood
Southwood's Stores
Hill Crest
Hertfordshire
HR21 5GN

Dear Mr Southwood

I have recently applied for a job as a clerical assistant at Timberlake Supplies in Lockdean, and I would very much like to be able to put your name forward as a reference both for myself and for the quality of my work.

As this will be my first full-time job, the company is keen to have some confirmation of my work experience. Having been employed by you as a Saturday assistant for the past year, I am hoping that you will, very kindly, be able to supply this.

I very much enjoyed working at Southwood's, and I believe that you were satisfied with the standard that I achieved while I was with you. I hope, therefore, that you will be able to write a suitable letter, for which I would be very grateful.

Yours sincerely

Anne Martin

From a friend

- Shelley is e-mailing a friend to ask her if she is willing to supply a character reference should her prospective employers ask for one.

- The tone of the letter is much more informal than the preceding ones. Shelley, however still puts the same points across.
- She says what the work is, and compares it to the work that she is doing now, so that Karen will have some idea of what she needs to write in the reference.
- She says why she has chosen Karen, reminds her of how long they have known each other, and suggests that she expects a reasonable reference from her.
- Shelley makes it clear that she is asking Karen for the character reference – what Shelley is like as a person – and that her current employer will be supplying the work reference.
- She closes by expressing her gratitude in an informal manner that suits a letter to a friend.

References
Shelley Cox [scox@anyisp.co.uk]
To: kmullholland@myisp.co.uk

Dear Karen

I have just applied for a job as care assistant at the residential home here. The work involves looking after the elderly and infirm, and seeing to their everyday needs. It's pretty much what I'm doing at the moment, but the conditions and pay are a lot better.

The Home has asked me to supply two references, and I am writing to you to ask if you would be willing for me to give them your name for the personal reference – I shall be asking my current employers for the other one.

Having known each other since we were at college together, I hope you can say by now whether or not I'm reasonably honest and law-abiding! I needn't tell you how grateful I would be.

Yours

Shelley

16

Answering job offers

General points

Congratulations, they have offered you the job.

Now you have to decide whether you want to:

- accept the job;
- decline the offer outright;
- decline the offered job, but ask to continue to be considered in the future.

Take a little time to think through your decision. Organisations will expect you to reply promptly but not necessarily by return of post.

You may want to consider the following points and compare them, both with your current position and with your ideal job:

- the duties and responsibilities of the new job;
- the pay and conditions, including perks and bonuses;
- the current state and likely future prospects of the company;
- the opportunities for development and promotion;
- the culture and environment of the new company.

Finally, when your job search has been successful and you have been offered the job that you want, you will need to write a letter of resignation to your current employer.

End on a positive note, and tell them how much you have enjoyed working for them. You may need their help and advice, or a reference, some day.

What you need to get across

Think about including these points in your letter:

- the job title and any reference number of the position;
- your acceptance or rejection of the offer;
- if accepting:
  - your understanding of the detailed terms and conditions of the offer if you have discussed them at this stage;
  - your pleasure in accepting the job;
- if rejecting:
  - your reasons for rejecting the offer if you feel this is appropriate;
  - your regrets and good wishes.

Accepting the offer

- You can see the covering letter that Andrew wrote in Chapter 5, *Answering advertised vacancies*.
- His application has been successful, and Ross College have offered him the position of Accommodation and Welfare Manager.
- He is accepting the post, and writes to confirm this, along with the starting date discussed at his interview.
- He includes a short paragraph on a more personal note, which will set a friendly tone for his working relationship with Ross College from the outset.

5 Windmill Court
Sellingsby
Birmingham
BM19 3JK

Tel: 0000 000 0000

4 September 2008

Ms J K Allison
Head of Personnel
Ross College
Warwickshire
WW11 2DC

Dear Ms Allison

Ref: UER/3/AO, Accommodation and Welfare Officer

Thank you for your letter of 2 September 2008. I am delighted to accept your offer of the above position and confirm that I will be able to start, as provisionally agreed, on 1 October 2008 in time for the beginning of the academic year.

May I say how much I am looking forward to working at Ross College, and I hope that this will be the start of a long and rewarding working relationship.

Yours sincerely

Andrew Patterson

Declining the offer

- Andrew has also been offered a job at the St Bernard's Housing Trust.
- He has, however, already accepted the position at Ross College, and this offer is not sufficiently attractive to persuade him to change his mind.
- He writes to them declining their offer, and explaining his reasons why. Andrew feels that they have given him a lot of

their time and attention and that they deserve more than just a straight 'no thanks'.

- He also tells them how much he appreciates their interest in him, and ends on a friendly note, wishing them well for the future.
- As well as being polite, Andrew also wants to maintain the good relationship that he has built up with them. He may need their help and advice at some time in the future.

5 Windmill Court
Sellingsby
Birmingham
BM19 3JK

Tel: 0000 000 0000

8 September 2008

Dr Henry Newell
Principal Officer
St Bernard's Housing Trust
Westwell
Birmingham
BM3 4WA

Dear Dr Newell

Thank you for your letter of 6 September 2008 offering me the position of Housing Officer for the St Bernard Housing Trust.

Unfortunately I have, after some consideration, decided to accept a position with Ross College as Accommodation and Welfare Officer. I will, therefore, have to decline your offer.

I appreciate the time and attention you have given my application, and I enjoyed my visit to the Trust very much. I had an interesting morning meeting everyone and seeing the work that you do.

May I wish you and the Trust every success in the future.

Yours sincerely

Andrew Patterson

Declining the offer but asking to be kept on record

- Allison wrote to a number of different organisations. Her letter can be seen in Chapter 6, *Speculative letters*.
- These letters led to a number of visits to companies for further discussions. Allison learned a lot about the employment situation in her particular field.
- Tiverton Financial have written back, following one of these meetings, to offer Allison a job in their accounts department.
- Allison is interested in working for this company, having been impressed by what she saw at the meeting. However, she has weighed up her requirements against what the job is offering, and has decided that it would not be in her interests to accept it.
- She therefore takes the risk of turning down this particular job, but asks to be kept on file and considered for other, more senior, jobs that might come up.
- Allison gives her reason for declining this particular offer. She states quite clearly that she is looking for a more senior position.
- There's a possibility that Tiverton will no longer be interested in Allison after she turns down their offer, but equally there is a chance that they will be. Allison loses nothing by asking.
- She closes on a positive note, saying how much she enjoyed her visit to them.

Ash Cottage
Tovey Lane
Tillington
Berkshire
BR17 4DF

Tel: 00000 000000

4 May 2008

Ms Dawn Hulpert
Personnel Manager
Tiverton Financial
Edward's Court
Hazel Ridge
Berkshire
BR9 6VH

Dear Ms Hulpert

Thank you for your letter of 3 May 2008 offering me the position of Administration Assistant in your Accounts Department.

After careful consideration, I have decided to decline the offer of this specific post. I would, however, still be interested in being considered for any more senior positions that you may have in the future, and request that you keep my name and details on file accordingly.

I greatly appreciate the time and attention you have given me and I enjoyed my visit to Tiverton Financial very much. I had an interesting time meeting everyone and seeing the work that you do.

Yours sincerely

Allison Tripp

Letter of resignation to current employer

- Ross has been offered the job of delivery representative, and has accepted it.
- You can see his original letter of application in Chapter 10, *Troubleshooting*.
- He now needs to write his letter of resignation to his current employer. Ross has already told Simon Jake, informally, that he has another job and will be leaving, but Simon will still need to have written confirmation.
- Ross tells him he is working out the full period of his notice, one month, and he includes the date he will be starting at his new job.
- He also says where he will be working and what he will be doing. This is not absolutely necessary, but it could be useful to the company for their records.
- Ross includes a paragraph on a more personal note, thanking Hogg Supplies for their help in the past. Again, this is not strictly necessary, but it will leave a good impression of Ross with the company should he need their help and advice in the future.

9 Old Meadow
East Inglestone
Gloucestershire
GL9 1VB

Tel: 00000 000000

16 January 2009

Mr Simon Jake
Manager
Hogg Supplies
Park Row
Inglestone
Gloucestershire
GL18 8NT

Dear Mr Jake

I am writing to you to confirm my resignation from Hogg Supplies as Delivery Driver.

I have accepted a position as Delivery Representative with Weber Foods plc, and will be starting with them on 23 February 2009 following my statutory period of notice here.

May I say how much I have enjoyed the past five years, and how grateful I am for the opportunity and experience you have given me during this time. I have made good friends here and I am sorry to be leaving, but this is a chance that I would be foolish to let pass.

I wish you and the company continuing success in the future.

Yours sincerely

Ross Walker

17

CVs and application forms

CVs

A curriculum vitae (CV) is a summary of your educational and working life, also sometimes called a career history, or a résumé.

The purpose of a CV is to illustrate clearly to a potential employer that you have the skills and experience required for the job that you want. Like a letter, the aim of a CV is to get you an interview with that potential employer.

Planning your CV – points to remember

- **Keep it short.** The ideal length for a CV is no more than one or two A4-sized pages.
- **Make sure that it's easy to read.** Your CV should always be printed, never handwritten. It needs to be well laid out with wide margins, clear section headings and information organised in a logical, easy-to-follow format. Keep in mind that it could be scanned into a computer data bank. A clear, simple, easy to read layout is essential. Do not use staples and do not fold it – use an A4 envelope to send your CV and covering letter.

- **Look at it from the employer's point of view.** An employer is looking for certain things in a potential employee, in particular that they:
  - can perform the specific skills of the job;
  - have experience relevant to the job;
  - have the right personal qualities for the job;
  - have an understanding of the particular problems of the job.

  Make sure you clearly understand the skills, experience, personal qualities and problems associated with the job you are aiming for.
- **Match your skills and experience to those required by the job.** Your *relevant* experience and achievements are the most important things to put in your CV.
- **State your accomplishments and achievements clearly.** Employers have neither the time nor patience to search out the information for themselves. They should be able to see at a glance exactly what you are offering. Spell out your achievements – a CV is not the place for false modesty.
- **Keep the wording simple and direct.** Stick to clear, unambiguous, factual statements.
- **Avoid unnecessary personal details.** The less irrelevant information there is on the page, the more your achievements will stand out – and it's these, after all, that the employer is most interested in. Unless they are strictly relevant, you can leave out the following items of information:
  - nationality;
  - gender;
  - maiden name;
  - number and ages of children;
  - partner's occupation;
  - religious affiliation;
  - age;
  - previous salary.

- **Avoid information that shows you in a negative light.** Never lie on a CV, but always put things in the most positive way you can.
- **Make sure that your CV is well presented.** Check spelling and grammar thoroughly. Ensure that the final result is well printed on plain white, good-quality paper, and looks professional.

What goes into a CV?

Individual CVs will be different depending on the person, their career, the stage reached in that career and so on. However, the majority of CVs contain the following elements, although the order in which they appear, and the emphasis given to each, is flexible.

- **Heading.** Start your CV with your name, home address, telephone number and e-mail address. If your CV runs on to a second page, put your name at the top of this page too.
- **Employment experience.** Names of employers, dates of employment, appointments and responsibilities. Employment history is usually shown in reverse chronological order starting with your most recent, and therefore most relevant, job.
- **Achievements.** Employers are keen to see what you have achieved in your previous positions. Relate your achievements to your work. Include areas such as increased productivity; increased sales or profits; improved customer relations; reduced staff turnover; improved design; increased efficiency; improved employee relations; increased public profile, etc. Aim to convey the benefits of what you have done.
- **Education and qualifications.** Unless you have recently left school or college, when a full academic record may be relevant, include only your highest academic qualifications and the subjects in which you gained them. Follow with any

professional qualifications, vocational qualifications, relevant training, or further *relevant* educational achievements.

- **Additional skills.** Include any skills or talents that have a general use, such as:
  - language skills – defined as either conversational or fluent;
  - IT skills – name packages used, for example Word, Access, Excel;
  - full, clean driving licence;
  - first-aid training.
- **Hobbies and interests.** Not always included. If they are, choose no less than two and no more than four. Pick interests and pastimes that complement and enhance your skills and experience.
- **References.** It is usual these days to simply state 'available on request' rather than to give actual names and addresses on the CV.
- **Optional extras.** Add these to your CV if they help to bring out your relevant skills and aptitudes more strongly. They can include:
  - *personal profile* – a short statement of not more than 30 words or so outlining your main attributes and key characteristics;
  - *career aim* – a concise account, again no more than 30 words, showing your career aims and objectives in a planned and logical manner.

Drafting your CV

Your finished CV should:

- be attractive;
- be easy to read;

- be easy to understand;
- present your skills, strengths and achievements clearly;
- encourage the reader to want to meet you.

The layout of your CV, the way it is arranged on the page, is important. Wide margins and clear spacing can emphasise information and help to put the message across. Paragraph length and spacing are also important – your CV should look easy to read. If your CV runs to two pages, put the most important information on the first page.

CV checklist

Having drawn up your CV, check the following points:

- Is the layout clear and easy to read?
- Do the relevant points stand out?
- Is the language clear and understandable?
- Are accomplishments and achievements emphasised?
- Can the reader see what is being offered at a glance? They shouldn't have to search for information.
- Is it free of irrelevant details?
- Is it free of qualifying words such as 'fairly', 'usually', 'hopefully', etc?
- Does a positive picture of you emerge?
- Is it well printed and professional looking?

See Chapter 3, *Online letters*, for details of the e-mailed CV.

Application forms

Application forms are designed to obtain information in a way that is standard for every applicant. Their major drawback is that they don't allow you the flexibility to present that information the way you want. In addition, they are sometimes poorly designed with the wrong-sized boxes for answers.

When filling in application forms bear in mind the following points:

- Always make a copy to fill in first before copying your answers on to the original. Keep the copy together with the original advert. It will be useful when you are called to the interview.
- Read the instructions very carefully. Are they asking for block capitals? Black ink? Work history in reverse order?
- Fill in all the boxes. If the question isn't relevant to you, put N/A for 'not applicable'.
- As with a CV or letter, make the information that you include relevant to the job in question.
- Leave out irrelevant information.
- Avoid saying 'see CV' – it looks lazy. Write the information, in full, on the form.
- Most application forms have a box at the end for you to include additional information in support of your application. This is your opportunity to include anything you haven't covered in the main body of the form. Use this, and your covering letter, to get your strongest points across and highlight your most relevant skills and experience.
- Always include a covering letter highlighting your chief points.
- Be positive and assertive about your skills and achievements.
- Never lie on the form – you can be dismissed if you are employed on the strength of a deliberately false application.

Many of the same rules apply for online application forms. Specific things to keep in mind are:

- Don't fill in the form and click send without giving it the same care and consideration you would any other application. Check spelling carefully as there probably won't be a spellcheck facility. To avoid errors, cut and paste your plain-text CV (see Chapter 3) into the form where possible.
- Make full use of any hints, tips and advice the site offers.
- Fill in all the boxes – incomplete forms are often not accepted for submission.

Sending it off

Before sending off your application, make sure that you have the name of the recipient, their job title or position, and the full address of the company including the postcode.

There is usually a closing date for applications. If this date allows you some time for research into the company and the job, then use it to the full. Make sure, though, that your application reaches them well within the allotted time, and allow for postal delays. Applications received after the deadline are rarely considered unless the circumstances are exceptional.

Finally

When sending finished forms or your CV to potential employers, check the following points:

- Include a covering letter written specifically with the needs of that employer in mind.
- Send the completed form or CV and letter, unfolded, in a white A4-size envelope.
- Send it by first-class post.
- Send it to a named individual within the company.

Improving a CV: Before

CURRICULUM VITAE

CANDIDATE:	DIANE WALKER
AGE:	40
DATE OF BIRTH:	12/6/68
NATIONALITY:	BRITISH
MARITAL STATUS:	DIVORCED
CHILDREN:	JAMES – 12 THOMAS – 16
EDUCATION	
1979–1984 Sheerside Secondary School	Obtained passes in: English Maths
1984–1985 South London College	Retail and Retail Display course: Day release Grade 1 pass
1985–1988 South London College	French evening class: Pass
EMPLOYMENT HISTORY	
2007–present Eastley Training Centre	Clerical Skills course: Typing, Word Processing, Office Administration.
2004–2007 Friends Assurance Association	General office administration
2001–2004 Keyline Retail	Supervising staff Attending to customers

1989–1992 Scottish Finance Co	Accounting Customer contact
1985–1989 United Insurance Ltd	Office administration, Invoicing, Bookkeeping
1984–1985 Dessarts Ltd	Shop Assistant, Trainee Display Assistant

HOBBIES AND INTERESTS
I enjoy music, dancing, keep fit, crosswords, etc and was a keen
member of the PTA.

Improving a CV: After

<u>DIANE WALKER</u>
83 Draycot Place,
Eastley, Surrey SR1 2AA
Telephone: 00000 000000
e-mail: walkerdi@anyisp.uk

Personal Profile

An experienced administrator and office manager with an extensive knowledge of business practices, especially in accounting, bookkeeping and inventory control. A good communicator, who has demonstrated a high degree of initiative and self motivation, and enjoys the challenge of a busy, demanding work environment. Conscientious, with the ability to maintain a consistently high standard of work under pressure. A good team member and leader.

Key Skills and Achievements

- Supervising staff
- Implementing standard procedures accurately
- Prioritising workload
- Analysing and rectifying errors

- Conversational French
- Computer Skills – Word
Access
Excel

Career History

2007–present	**Eastley Training Centre** NVQ level 3 – Clerical Skills course: Administration and Supervision. Advanced course to update and expand office management skills.
2004–2007	**Friends Assurance Association** Office Administration – Responsible for all collation and administration of documentation and records. Also dealt with all queries to the department, and the organisation of data within the department.
2001–2004	**Keyline Retail** Section Manager – Supervising staff and attending to customers in busy city-centre store. Responsible for daily administration of section, including stock control, section turnover, and customer complaints.
1989–1992	**Scottish Finance Co** Office Administration – Responsible for analysing and rectifying accounting errors in customer accounts.
1985–1989	**United Insurance Ltd** Office Administration – Carried out administrative work of department, including processing payroll, co-ordinating work schedules, invoicing and ordering.
1984–1985	**Dessarts Ltd** Display and retail assistant.

Do-it-yourself section

This chapter contains:

- positive statements and action words;
- character profiles;
- career objectives;
- ideas for opening gambits.

Use the ideas here as inspiration for your own letters.

Positive statements

Positive statements are useful for compiling letters and CVs. They can be divided into:

- positive characteristics;
- action words;
- positive descriptions.

Positive characteristics

These words describe personal attributes often seen as positive and beneficial in the workplace.

Choose the words that you feel describe you best, and use them when describing yourself in your letters.

Able Accurate Adaptable Adroit
Adventurous Alert Ambitious Analytical
Appreciative Articulate Assertive Astute

Bilingual Bright

Calm Capable Competent Confident
Consistent Co-operative Creative

Decisive Dedicated Dependable Diligent
Diplomatic

Educated Effective Efficient Energetic
Enthusiastic Experienced Expert

Fast Firm Fit Flexible
Friendly

Gregarious

Hardworking Healthy Honest Human
Humane

Imaginative Independent Informed Ingenious
Innovative Intelligent Inventive

Knowledgeable

Literate Loyal

Mature Methodical Motivated Multilingual

Non-smoking

Objective Open-minded Organised Outgoing
Outstanding

Patient	People-oriented	Perceptive	Persistent
Personable	Pioneering	Poised	Practical
Principled	Productive	Professional	Proficient
Punctual			
Qualified	Quick	Quick-thinking	
Rational	Ready	Realistic	Reliable
Resourceful	Responsible	Robust	
Scrupulous	Self-assured	Self-confident	Self-motivated
Self-reliant	Sensitive	Serious	Shrewd
Skilled	Smart	Spirited	Stable
Strong	Successful	Supportive	
Tactful	Talented	Tenacious	Thorough
Thoughtful	Trained	Trustworthy	
Versatile	Vigorous		
Well-educated	Well-groomed	Willing	Witty
Young	Youthful		

Action words

These are positive, active words that you can use to describe your achievements.

Accelerated	Accessed	Achieved	Acquired
Acted	Administered	Advised	Analysed
Appointed	Appraised	Arranged	Assigned
Assisted	Attended		
Booked	Broadened	Budgeted	
Checked	Coached	Collaborated	Communicated
Competed	Compiled	Completed	Conceived
Conducted	Consulted	Contributed	Controlled
Co-ordinated	Correlated	Created	

Delegated	Demonstrated	Designed	Determined
Developed	Devised	Diagnosed	Directed
Doubled			
Edited	Effected	Eliminated	Enabled
Established	Evaluated	Executed	Exercised
Expanded	Expedited	Explored	
Facilitated	Fostered	Formulated	Founded
Generated	Guided		
Handled	Harmonised	Headed	Helped
Hired			
Identified	Implemented	Improved	Increased
Initiated	Installed	Instituted	Instructed
Interacted	Invented	Investigated	
Launched	Led		
Maintained	Managed	Marketed	Mentored
Monitored	Motivated		
Negotiated			
Opened	Operated	Organised	Oversaw
Participated	Performed	Pinpointed	Pioneered
Planned	Prepared	Presented	Processed
Produced	Programmed	Promoted	Proposed
Provided	Purchased		
Recommended	Recorded	Recruited	Reduced
Reorganised	Reported	Represented	Researched
Resolved	Restored	Restructured	Reviewed
Revised			
Saved	Scheduled	Secured	Selected
Set up	Shaped	Sold	Solved
Structured	Supervised		
Taught	Tested	Trained	

Upgraded Used Utilised

Visualised

Won Wrote

Positive descriptions

As well as using positive words for your characteristics and achievements, positive statements also suggest ways to describe your strengths.

Instead of saying 'I am good at…', you could say:

- skilled at…
- a skilful…
- a degree of ability in…
- very good at…
- extremely good at…
- exceptional at…
- adept at…
- an expert in…
- excelling at…
- with the ability to…
- competence in…
- an experienced…
- a deft…
- a talent for…
- familiar with…
- qualified to…

For example:

- I am skilled at facilitating the exchange of ideas.
- I am a skilful communicator.
- I have a high degree of ability in computer programming.
- I am adept at promoting policy changes.
- I am very good at handling a variety of tasks efficiently.
- I am exceptional at motivating large or small groups.
- I have a talent for budget projection.
- I am familiar with a wide range of software.
- I am qualified to assess retail training up to NVQ level 3.

Personal profiles

Personal profiles are brief, thumbnail sketches used in letters and CVs to get across an idea of the sort of person you are. It is an opportunity to put across your personal strengths and qualities.

The following are examples of short, one-paragraph character sketches:

- Open-minded, outgoing and resourceful, with an enquiring mind and optimistic outlook, I have a sound background in Human Resource Administration. I possess a good sense of humour and the ability to develop and motivate others. This, coupled with the ability to communicate comfortably at all levels, ensures good teamwork and an energetic and productive working environment.
- I have over 15 years' experience of training and development, with seven years at senior management level. I can communicate with all levels of staff and clients, and have an excellent track record in Quality Management. I successfully

combine a hands-on style of management with a proven ability to plan and deliver training to the highest standard.

- I am a professional sales manager with an unusual breadth of experience in the international market. Dependable and energetic, I have the ability to motivate and direct a work-force to meet its targets and objectives. I always endeavour to achieve the highest standards in every undertaking.
- I am an innovative and intelligent engineer who has designed and installed systems for a variety of clients. I am adept at working effectively with a multi-disciplined team at senior level, and have many years experience of under-standing and evaluating problems in my line of work.
- I am a mature sales executive with many years' experience of quality food products. An expert at selling to leading manufacturers nationwide, I am skilled at building customer loyalty. In addition, I have developed, through many years' experience, a high level of management and organisational skills.

When you compile a personal profile, include some or all of the following areas. Give them a greater or lesser degree of emphasis, depending on what you wish to highlight, but always include factual information about your skills and experience, not just your opinion of your personal strengths or qualities:

- **Experience,** such as:
  - five years in sales management;
  - wide experience of...;
  - a good working knowledge of...;
  - an excellent track record in... .
- **Skills**, such as:
  - management skills;
  - communication skills;
  - organisational skills;
  - problem-solving and decision-making skills;
  - design skills.

- **Personal qualities,** such as:
  - self-motivated;
  - creative;
  - hardworking;
  - reliable;
  - innovative;
  - organised;
  - adaptable.
- **Personal strengths,** such as:
  - work well under pressure;
  - eye for detail;
  - enjoy challenge;
  - good sense of humour;
  - an effective, disciplined worker.

See other examples of key words in Chapter 3, *Online letters*.

Career objectives

Career objectives are brief statements about what you plan to do. Include them in a letter or CV to give an idea of the sort of position you are looking for.

This is particularly useful when you are making a speculative approach to companies. It helps them if they have a clear impression of what you want.

When sending a letter in answer to an advertised vacancy, make sure that your career objectives fit the ones in the advertisement. The following are examples of short, one-paragraph career objectives:

- I am a competent, highly motivated project leader seeking a position where I can put my enthusiasm and experience to good use in an environment where research produces solid end results.

- I am a marketing professional, interested in all types of communication. I now wish to focus on a career in public relations where I can put the skills and experience I have acquired to their most effective use.
- As a chartered engineer with 10 years' experience in management, I am looking for a senior position where my knowledge and skill will make a significant contribution towards corporate goals.
- I am an engineering graduate with a keen interest in information technology, seeking a career in computing. My special interests are in the scientific and industrial fields, where my background in problem-solving would be an advantage.
- A fast, flexible, quick-thinking administration assistant, I am looking for the opportunity to make use of my arts education in the field of publishing.
- As a systems analyst with a background in the finance sector, I am interested in applying information technology to the improvement of company efficiency.

When compiling a career objective, include the following points:

- Say what you do – offer a job title or a job description.
- Include your key strengths.
- Say where you're coming from – your background and experience.
- Say what you're aiming for – how you want to use your skills and experience.

Opening gambits

Opening gambits are used in letters, especially speculative letters, to give a reason for writing at this particular time. They serve as an introduction for your skills and experience, and allow you to say how these could be of benefit to the company. Ideally they should be topical, positive, relevant, and interesting.

The following are examples of good opening gambits:

- I hear with interest that your company is intending to set up a new export division at the start of the year. It occurs to me that you may have an opening for an experienced export clerk...
- I understand from Ellen Edwards that you will shortly be opening a new freight-handling department. My first-hand experience of freight forwarding includes...
- Having noticed the extensive new building programme at your Petersfield Road site, I was interested to learn from this evening's *Lewes Gazette* of your plans for an advanced warehouse and storage facility. As a warehouse manager of many years' experience...
- Your company profile published in today's *Business Week* indicates that you are proposing to expand your Agrochemical division. I believe that my specific experience in this area could be of benefit to you...
- Recent information on your website suggests that your company is relocating its claims department from Harlow to Swindon. This being the case...
- I was most interested to see your recent press campaign highlighting your advances in fibre optics. As a fibre-optics engineer qualified to BS3009 standard...
- I met Paul Harris at the recent *Business Software Now* Exhibition, and he suggested that I contact you concerning your expansion into desktop publishing.